Cambridge Elements ≡

Elements in Publishing and Book Culture
edited by
Samantha Rayner
University College London
Leah Tether
University of Bristol

LONDON AND THE MODERNIST BOOKSHOP

Matthew Chambers
University of Warsaw

CAMBRIDGE
UNIVERSITY PRESS

CAMBRIDGE
UNIVERSITY PRESS

University Printing House, Cambridge CB2 8BS, United Kingdom

One Liberty Plaza, 20th Floor, New York, NY 10006, USA

477 Williamstown Road, Port Melbourne, VIC 3207, Australia

314–321, 3rd Floor, Plot 3, Splendor Forum, Jasola District Centre,
New Delhi – 110025, India

79 Anson Road, #06–04/06, Singapore 079906

Cambridge University Press is part of the University of Cambridge.

It furthers the University's mission by disseminating knowledge in the pursuit of
education, learning, and research at the highest international levels of excellence.

www.cambridge.org
Information on this title: www.cambridge.org/9781108708692
DOI: 10.1017/9781108769853

First published 2020

A catalogue record for this publication is available from the British Library.

ISBN 978-1-108–70869-2 Paperback
ISSN 2514-8524 (online)
ISSN 2514-8516 (print)

London and the Modernist Bookshop

Elements in Publishing and Book Culture

DOI: 10.1017/9781108769853
First published online: April 2020

Matthew Chambers
University of Warsaw
Author for correspondence: matthewjosephchambers@gmail.com

ABSTRACT: The modernist bookshop, best exemplified by Sylvia Beach's Shakespeare & Co. and Harold Monro's Poetry Bookshop, has received scant attention outside of these more prominent examples. This Element will review how bookshops like David Archer's on Parton Street (London) in the 1930s were sites of distribution, publication, and networking. Parton Street, which also housed Lawrence & Wishart publishers and a briefly vibrant literary scene, will be approached from several contexts as a way of situating the modernist bookshop within both the book trade and the literary communities that it interacted with and made possible.

KEYWORDS: modernism, print cultures, book history, cultural politics, Popular Front

ISBNs: 9781108708692 (PB), 9781108769853 (OC)
ISSNs: 2514-8524 (online), 2514-8516 (print)

Contents

1 Introduction: Modernist Bookshops

I got out at Holborn Station and asked the way to Parton Street. No one had heard of it. Michael Roberts had mentioned Red Lion Square. I found my way to that pleasant quiet garden, shaded by London planes, the trunks patterned with large mosaic. He had mentioned the LCC Central School of Art, and there it was, on the corner. And there was Parton Street, narrow alley joining the square to Theobald's Road.

I found it in the end because of the gay display of posters advertising the *Daily Worker*, *Russia Today*, and *USSR in Construction*. ... In 1933 outside [David] Archer's bookshop were racks of unfamiliar and exciting periodicals. ... Inside the shop rows and rows of poets' slim volumes. – Maurice Carpenter, *Rebel in the Thirties*

Parton Street is a place-name evocative of 1930s literary London. Located a little more than two blocks southeast of the British Museum where Bloomsbury meets Holborn, the street connected Red Lion Square to Theobald's Road near Holborn Station. For a time, the street gave its name to a community of poets, artists, and activists moved by W. H. Auden, Dylan Thomas, surrealism, the Communist Party of Great Britain (CPGB), and the Spanish Civil War. David Archer's bookshop at 4 Parton Street, most famous for publishing Dylan Thomas's first book, brought all those individuals and interests together. In fact, along with Archer's, two other vital modernist institutions gave shape to the scene: a publisher and a cafe. And while publishers and cafes have been well considered within modernist studies, bookshops have generally been overlooked. This Element will use Parton Street as a case study to explore the role of the bookshop within the networks of modernist literary production. Even if Archer's stands as one example of what Huw Osborne has termed the "modernist bookshop," the shop's relationship to Lawrence & Wishart publishers next door and Meg's Cafe across the way presents an opportunity to consider how modernist bookshops existed as part of the world of literary publishing and socializing.

Yet, Parton Street did not simply function as a convenient marker for a congestion of activity but formed through cultural and geographical forces that made such activity possible. The street, as I have noted, existed on the edges of Bloomsbury, itself a place of unclear geographical borders and of overloaded cultural significance. Sara Blair, approaching the "geocultural landscape" of Bloomsbury, has argued that it was "not place alone but the generation of a host of tactics ... that comprise[d] both material Bloomsbury and 'Bloomsbury', at once a habitat and the forms of belonging to it."[1] Archer's bookshop on a specific street, in a specific neighborhood, drew from its location and constructed an idea of itself embedded in its environs. As Section 2 will demonstrate, David Archer's choice of Parton Street for the bookshop and, indeed, the idea for the bookshop itself were very much rooted in local activism.

Before we arrive at the bookshop's origins, we should attend to the "forms of belonging" that made Parton Street a meaningful space. To accomplish this, I will first take a slight detour over to Charing Cross Road and the bookshops found there in the decade before Archer's opened its doors. In particular, I want to focus on Henderson's at 66 Charing Cross Road, which, from 1919 to 1920, published *Coterie*. The journal featured an impressive number of American and British poets and advertised its stock in a section in the back of each issue entitled "At the Bomb Shop" (as the shop was more familiarly known).[2] *Coterie* doubled as a literary publication and advertisement for the bookshop, as did *Poetry Review* for Harold Monro's Poetry Bookshop at the same time. The networks these journals generated for their bookshops extended beyond their locations in London and also rendered the poetry they published synonymous with the shops' locations. *Coterie*'s name speaks to the coming together as "habitat and forms of belonging." Jennifer Wicke,

---

[1] S. Blair, "Local Modernity, Global Modernism: Bloomsbury and the Places of the Literary," *ELH* 71.3 (Fall 2004), pp.815–16. An example Blair gives of what made those "host of tactics" for progressive individuals possible was the area's infrastructure: she takes the easy divisibility of the signature Georgian townhouse for single living as a determining feature (820), a feature also present and meaningful on Parton Street as it contained similar buildings.

[2] For full electronic reproductions of *Coterie* with some more contextualizing history of the periodical, visit *The Modernist Journals Project* at http://mod journ.org/render.php?view=mjp_object&id=coterie.catalog

also writing on Bloomsbury, has argued that a coterie as well defined as Bloomsbury not only consumed "in a concerted effort of knowledge, taste, and power" but also presented the coterie lifestyle itself as desirable for consumption, producing a "coterie of and for consumption, a force within the market that made a market."[3] Circling back to Parton Street, as all the various memoirs of the shop attest, it briefly held up a desirable coterie lifestyle to be consumed, even if it remains difficult to explain exactly what it was.

To get at the unique form of a bookshop like Archer's within modernist print cultures, we can turn to the journals and literary collections it sold for an analogy. If, for example, *Coterie*'s title speaks to a form of belonging, the journal's format points to its plurality. Osborne, who has edited the only extended analysis of modernist bookshops to date, sees bookshops framed similarly, likening them to the anthologies, periodicals, and miscellanies of the time. Modernist bookshops are places where "authors, readers, representations, interpretations, production, and dissemination cohere in diversely unpredictable acts of intellectual and material change."[4] Approached in this way, modernist bookshops resemble collections such as periodicals or anthologies. As a kind of provisional institution or "authored work," to borrow Jeremy Braddock's term, modernist bookshops, like the modernist collections of the gallery or anthology he concerns himself with, "exist not simply for the sake of their individual works; they are also systems with meanings in themselves."[5] To take on board Braddock's concept of the modernist collection for bookshops means that attention must be paid to the shop's stock, the bookseller, finances, customers, locale, and scene as determining elements in a literary community.

---

[3] J. Wicke, "Coterie Consumption: Bloomsbury, Keynes, and Modernism as Marketing," in K. J. Dettmar and S. Watt (eds.), *Marketing Modernisms: Self-Promotion, Canonization, Rereading* (Ann Arbor: University of Michigan Press, 1996), p. 116.

[4] H. Osborne, "Introduction: Openings," in H. Osborne (ed.), *The Rise of the Modernist Bookshop: Books and the Commerce of Culture in the Twentieth Century* (Farnham: Ashgate Publishing Ltd., 2015), p. 6.

[5] J. Braddock, *Collecting as Modernist Practice* (Baltimore: The Johns Hopkins University Press, 2012), p.6.

Braddock, like many others writing on modernist institutions, refers to Lawrence Rainey's *Institutions of Modernism* when establishing his own sense of a "provisional institution." Rainey, in an oft-quoted passage building on Jurgen Habermas's theorization of the eighteenth-century public sphere, argued that "modernism, poised at the cusp of that transformation of the public sphere, responded with a tactical retreat into a divided world of patronage, collecting, speculation, and investment, a retreat that entailed the construction of an institutional counterspace, securing a momentary respite from a public realm increasingly degraded."[6] Braddock demurs, instead arguing that "[r]ather than constructing a regressive 'institutional counterspace', the modernist collection was figured as … a *provisional institution*, a mode of public engagement modeling future … relationships between audience and artwork."[7] What better place to build such relationships than a bookshop? Andrew Thacker, discussing the "public face of the modernist bookshop," argues that "[t]o run a bookshop which stocks experimental or

[6] L. Rainey, *Institutions of Modernism: Literary Elites and Public Culture* (New Haven: Yale University Press, 1998), p. 5.

[7] Braddock, *Collecting as Modernist Practice*, p. 3. Rainey's framing of modernist institutions has come under critique from several angles. Ronald Schleifer challenges Rainey's definition of institutions – "structures that interpose themselves between the individual and society" – for assuming the "'individual and society' to be more or less natural entities rather than examining how they are instituted by means of habits, transpersonal rules, and cultural formations." L. Rainey, *Institutions of Modernism*, p. 6. See also R. Schleifer, *A Political Economy of Modernism: Literature, Post-Classical Economics, and the Lower Middle-Class* (Cambridge: Cambridge University Press, 2018), p. 41. And more recently, John Xiros Cooper reminds us that Rainey limits what he means by institution to "small literary periodicals, literary presses, coteries and the like in the early years of the movement." J. X. Cooper, "Bringing the Modern to Market: The Case of Faber & Faber," in L. Jaillant (ed.), *Publishing Modernist Fiction and Poetry* (Edinburgh: Edinburgh University Press, 2019), p. 89. Patrick Collier takes issue with Rainey's conceptualization of how and where aesthetic evaluation occurs, arguing that Rainey is on "dubious ground … [for] suggesting that some alternative sphere might exist, or has existed, in which value is constructed in the absence of identifiable, competing interests." Collier, *Modern Print Artefacts*, p. 24.

avant-garde texts represents a direct engagement with a public culture of commerce," adding that "[m]odernist bookshops … appear to dwell both inside and outside the market, existing as part of the degraded public sphere and as spaces where counterpublic discourses might emerge."[8] A modernist bookshop, however radically posed, still ran a business in the book trade – it simply could not be viewed as a full retreat from the public realm.

I use Parton Street as an example in this Element to also foreground the role of the book trade on modernist bookshops and literary modernism. The focus here has been restricted to the 1930s, which, on the one hand, signifies along certain well-established lines within modernist studies, but the decade also saw important developments within the book trade that would have direct effects on bookshops and bookdealers. Most impactfully, the trade became more regulated following the Net Book Agreement (NBA) in 1901, but more so following a new emphasis on its enforcement in 1929. Broadly put, the NBA declared that publishers must sell new titles to all booksellers at the same net price, and, in turn, booksellers could not sell below the established net price.[9] As an agreement among members of the Publishers Association and the Booksellers Association, it created stability in the trade and gave smaller bookdealers fairer competitive terms with the larger outlets.[10] The NBA survived for decades to come, even while publishers

[8] A. Thacker, "'A True Magic Chamber': The Public Face of the Modernist Bookshop," *Modernist Cultures* 11.3 (2016), p. 434.

[9] Frederick Macmillan successfully experimented with net pricing in 1890 with Alfred Marshall's *The Principles of Economics*. M. Plant, *The English Book Trade; An Economic History of the Making and Sale of Books* (London: George Allen & Unwin Ltd., 1939), pp. 441–2. Coincidentally enough, Marshall was an important figure for David Archer while the latter was at Cambridge (see Section 3).

[10] The Booksellers Association was previously the Associated Booksellers of Great Britain and Ireland (1895), but I have retained its current and more commonly known name to avoid confusion, especially as this Element does not focus on the internal developments of the association. As for the NBA, to be sure its implementation was uneven and there were differing views over its benefits. Booksellers opposed more competitors and the resulting lower turnover, whereas publishers desired an expansion of outlets for distribution. R. J. Taraporevala, *Competition and Its Control in the British Book Trade, 1850–1939* (London: Pitman

like Basil Blackwell and G. S. Williams worried that a proliferation of booksellers would not increase overall sales for their firms but would instead introduce complexity into the trade.[11]

Another significant development – the modern paperback – sustained the trade during a period otherwise marked by a global economic depression and the aforementioned conservatism toward expanding competition. The modern paperback combined the old and unpopular paper-covered book with the new and cheap reprint series.[12] Lise Jaillant has argued that cheap reprint series not only expanded general readership but also helped circulate literary modernism, as figures like Virginia Woolf and James Joyce would be reprinted alongside other so-called middlebrow fare.[13] It is a claim heightened by a recent assertion that around one-third of the British reading public in the 1930s and 1940s owned paperbacks.[14]

There were other considerations for prospective bookdealers in the 1930s. Circulating libraries and book clubs were popular means of drawing clientele.[15] And the NBA gained influence after 1929 when it added

Publishing, 1973), p. 114. John Feather, who relies on Taraporevala for much of his NBA discussion, opens his chapter on "The Publishing Industry" with the declaration that the NBA "was the principal support upon which the whole structure of the British publishing industry rested for almost the whole of the twentieth century. J. Feather, *A History of British Publishing*, 2nd ed. (London: Routledge, 2006), p. 152. Thomas Joy, who was a prominent mid-century bookseller and commentator on the trade, argued that the NBA was an overall good for smaller bookdealers. T. Joy, *The Bookselling Business* (London: Pitman Publishing, 1974), p. 26.

[11] J. Barnes, *Free Trade in Books: A Study of the London Book Trade since 1800* (Oxford: Clarendon Press, 1964), pp. 152–3.

[12] Feather, *A History of British Publishing*, pp. 172–3.

[13] L. Jaillant, *Cheap Modernism*, p. 5.

[14] P. Mandler, "Good Reading for the Million: The 'Paperback Revolution' and the Co-Production of Academic Knowledge in Mid-Twentieth Century Britain and America," *Past and Present* 24.1 (August 2019), pp. 251–2. J. R. Evans, "The Promethean Society: A Survey," *Twentieth Century* 1 (March 1931), p. 23.

[15] I discuss circulating libraries in Section 3 in some depth, and book clubs in Section 4.

oversight to trade terms applications submitted to the Publishers Association by booksellers. In short, a small bookdealer like David Archer could enter a relatively stable market with some mitigation of risk.[16]

A bookshop like Archer's could conceivably get trade terms and expect some price protection in the market. But as Section 3 will show, the shop mainly relied on smaller firms for its stock. And those firms relied on small shops like Archer's for distribution. Publishers like Victor Gollancz Ltd., Hogarth Press, and Lawrence & Wishart advertised and distributed in narrower channels than their larger competitors. Advertisements might be bought in *The Times* but would more regularly be featured in the *Daily Worker*, *New Verse*, and *Left Review* and would sometimes direct the reader to a specific bookshop.[17] These relationships between bookdealers and publishers, as well as among bookdealers themselves, made the trade an intimate space. Jean-Luc Nancy captured this intimacy when he declared that a "bookstore is always found on the edge of a grand avenue that leads nowhere but from book to book."[18] This image, considered as a description of the trade, emphasizes both the localness of the bookshop and the interconnectedness of the book trade. Places like Archer's may not have always been on the main thoroughfares, but neither did they exist in a vacuum. There were more than sixty bookshops in Parton Street's W.C.1 postcode in 1934, fifty within a kilometer of Archer's. One brief example best underscores how this community of bookselling functioned: Ben Weinreb, who worked at Archer's and later became a well-established bookdealer in his own right, began his career as a book runner. Shops like Archer's would advertise that they could acquire

[16] Taraporevala, *Competition and Its Control*, pp. 137–9.

[17] For example, Nancy Cunard advertised her Hours Press in a circular noting in which shops her books were stocked (a strategy *Left Review* regularly employed in its back pages). For Cunard and the Hours Press, see N. Cunard, *These Were the Hours* (Carbondale: Southern Illinois University Press, 1969), p. 15. Hammill and Hussey, *Modernism's Print Cultures*, p. 109.

[18] J. L. Nancy, *On the Commerce of Thinking: Of Bookshops and Bookstores* (New York: Fordham University Press, 2009), p. 45.

titles available at other dealers across London in short periods of time, and runners like Weinreb would fetch them.[19]

To foreground the importance of place and network for a bookshop, this Element progresses as a series of close views at the individual addresses on Parton Street. Section 2, "Red Lion Square," examines the political activity at the South Place Ethical Society, as well as the forming of the Promethean Society, to both introduce how the adjoining Parton Street became a place for networking and examine how David Archer came to open a bookshop there. In Parton Street's prehistory, we have the blueprint for the literary and political activity that was to follow. Section 3, "4 Parton Street," details the bookshop opened there and its founder David Archer. This section has two central purposes: to examine the figure of the bookseller and to examine the varied lives and functions of a modernist bookshop. Section 4, "2 Parton Street," focuses on the publisher Lawrence & Wishart's early years (1936–9) at this address, especially its formal business partnership with the Workers' Bookshop and Collet's Bookshop, and less formal connection to the bookshop next door. This section also reviews Lawrence & Wishart's challenges partnering with the publisher Victor Gollancz on the influential Left Book Club to highlight the important role book clubs had in the identity of shops like Archer's in the 1930s. The Element concludes in "1 Parton Street and Beyond" with a discussion of Meg's Cafe and the difficulty of reconstructing the archives of modernist institutions, as well as a consideration of possible ways forward for the study of modernist bookshops with a review of some of Archer's contemporaries.

2 Red Lion Square

The origins of the Parton Street scene begin with David Archer's bookshop. But why did Archer open a bookshop on Parton Street? Why did he open a bookshop at all? The answer begins with the fact that the shop was opened as a Promethean Society venture. The story of the society itself is

---

[19] N. Barker, "Obituary: Ben Weinreb," *The Independent* (April 7, 1999), www.independent.co.uk/arts-entertainment/obituary-ben-weinreb-1085605.html [accessed January 12, 2019].

centered on Holborn and Red Lion Square. This section focuses on the formation of the Promethean Society to set up the intellectual and social background that shaped Archer's bookshop. In essence, the Promethean Society gave Archer's the identity that later attracted politically involved artists and writers. And Red Lion Square was an ideal space for the Promethean Society to establish itself.

As the statue of Fenner Brockway and a bust of Bertrand Russell that bookend the park in Red Lion Square attest, the square has been the site of much radical activity since the early twentieth century.[20] The South Place Ethical Society (SPES) moved to the newly built Conway Hall on Red Lion Square in the late 1920s and drew much of that activity.[21] Conway Hall was, and remains, a space devoted to the debate of religion and ethics and regularly holds concerts, talks, and study groups. The hall features lectures on literature, politics, and science, and the space serves as a meeting place for a myriad of groups and activities. But in its first years at the Red Lion Square address, it underwent a bit of an identity crisis. SPES had a close relationship with the Rationalist Press Association (RPA); in fact, two of SPES's appointed lecturers had been key RPA members (Joseph McCabe and Archibald Robertson). A junior RPA member, J. B. Coates, who also edited SPES's monthly publication, *Ethical Record*, openly challenged the RPA's focus in an August 1931 entry into the RPA's organ *Literary Guide*. This led to a failed leadership challenge within the RPA, but it left Coates

---

[20] Indeed the location has been no stranger to social protest: it is claimed that the exhumed corpse of Oliver Cromwell was held at an inn at Red Lion Fields the night before his second "execution." A. Fraser, *Cromwell: The Lord Protector* (New York: Grove Press, 1973), pp. 692–3. And later when that field was developed into a square in 1684, neighboring Gray's Inn inhabitants, protesting the loss of their view, battled the development's workers. D. Hayes, *East of Bloomsbury* Camden History Society, 1998), p. 13, In a quieter mode, a blue plaque at 17 Red Lion Square notes that Dante Gabriel Rossetti (1851), William Morris, and Sir Edward C. Burne-Jones (1856–9) lived there, formative years for Morris after student life at Oxford. F. MacCarthy, *William Morris: A Life of Our Time* (London: Faber and Faber, 1994), pp. 110–53.

[21] "Conway Hall: Beginnings," https://conwayhall.org.uk/ethical-society/beginnings

and figures like C. E. M. Joad motivated to found their own society.[22] Another incident compounded the administrative uncertainty during this time, when F. M. Overy, SPES secretary and manager, was found dead of an apparent suicide following a diagnosis of a terminal illness.[23] In fact, SPES's records of its early years at Conway Hall are scanty, suggesting some turmoil in its management, but it would remain an important address for progressive activists.

As it turned out, Coates was not alone in stirring generational controversy in his circles. In April 1930, E. M. Barraud wrote to the editor of *Everyman* complaining that columnists G. D. H. Cole and Liam Flaherty had been stoking up subversiveness without providing a path forward for people such as herself. In a frightening reveal of how isolated a woman with non-mainstream views could be made to feel in interwar Britain, she opined "[t]here must be dozens of people like myself who'd rather be dead right away than die by inches over a number of years."[24] She goes on to demand "I want to meet the rest of us."[25] Somewhat remarkably, she would get her wish. Over the next several months, *Everyman* published the responses under the banner "The Revolt of Youth"; by the summer, Barraud was joined by George Pendle and Jon Randell Evans in manifesto mode, arguing that they "want to fight against death" and insisted they were "not cranks bent upon forming an 'organization' ... [and were not] content to talk about Change, but [would] work changes in the world."[26] In the following issue, they appealed to interested individuals to help "form a loose association of small groups ... supplemented and co-ordinated by postal correspondence."[27] By the following March, this "loose association"

---

[22] B. Cooke, *The Blasphemy Depot: A Hundred Years of the Rationalist Press Association* (London: Rationalist Press Association, 2003), pp. 99–103.

[23] "Ethical Society Secretary Found Dead," *The Times* (August 16, 1932), p. 7. The *Ethical Record* paid tribute to Overy, noting he scouted the Red Lion Square address and advocated for SPES's move there (E.F.E. 1932, 2–3).

[24] E. M. Barraud, "The Revolt of Youth," *Everyman* 3.63 (April 10, 1930), p. 336.

[25] Barraud, "Revolt of Youth," 336.

[26] G. Pendle, J. R. Evans, E. M. Barraud, "The Revolt of Youth," *Everyman* 3.74 (June 26, 1930), p. 684.

[27] G. Pendle, J. R. Evans, E. M. Barraud, "The Revolt of Youth," *Everyman* 3.76 (July 10, 1930), p. 716.

had congealed into the Promethean Society, which announced itself in the form of the new journal *Twentieth Century*.

Leaving aside the journal for a moment, some attention should first be paid to how the004 Prometheans ended up on Red Lion Square. A few of its founding members lived in, or moved into, the neighborhood; by late 1931, Barraud's, Evans's, and Pendle's names, among others, began appearing as participants of a "study circle" at Conway Hall where they were listed as members of SPES by the end of spring 1932.[28] The study circle never formally declared itself as the Promethean Society. I would hazard to guess these were organizational meetings, as *Twentieth Century* never advertised the study circle either. More than being a curious detail, I believe it important that the Promethean Society privately sought some administrative center when its public pronouncements touted its heterogeneous, decentered formation and went so far as to hold the meetings of their various groups around London.[29]

---

[28] Evans, William Warbey, and Geoffrey Trease all lived within a few blocks of Red Lion Square. Twenty people joined SPES in April 1932, and the known Prometheans include Alec Craig, Evans, Joad, Archibald Robertson, Warbey, and Trease. Barraud joined in May and David Archer later. It is possible more of the names who joined in April were Prometheans as the number of memberships was unusually high that month for that period at SPES (typically between five and seven people), but I have been unable to confirm the other names as Prometheans.

[29] For example, its twice monthly general meetings were held at Gowerdene House (100–102 Gower Street) for some time, itself a hostel run by the National Holiday Touring Club Ltd. (NHTC), which had attempted to purchase the freehold from the University of London in 1931 when its lease was ending. When that bid failed, NHTC folded up and general meetings of the Promethean Society ceased at that address. Presumably, as the London address was advertised as a destination for "the benefit of Scotch and North county members," it was selected to accommodate non-London-based Prometheans. Email from Robert Winckworth, archives assistant at the University College London Special Collections, Archives & Records (August 21, 2018). See also *N.H.T.C.: Its Plans for 1931* (National Holiday Touring Club, Ltd., 1931).

The society's very construction has made accounting for its goals, accomplishments, and history difficult. There is no Promethean Society archive. No minutes of meetings, copies of talks, or correspondence survives. But perhaps it is more fitting to speak of its archive as uncollected, for, in addition to mentions in memoirs, we have the *Twentieth Century*. From our perspective looking back, the journal presents us with the textual register of the society's activities and necessarily becomes the center of what was an avowedly decentralized outfit. And for the stated focus of this Element, as the journal is the explanation for how David Archer's bookshop came to be on Parton Street, so it is to the journal we must turn. The common wisdom about *Twentieth Century* and the Promethean Society is that a group of individuals inspired by D. H. Lawrence, H. G. Wells, Karl Marx, and Sigmund Freud cobbled together a mess of progressive ideas that never went anywhere. The story of William Warbey and Geoffrey Trease seeking out Wells and the latter insisting they "must find a basis" informs this view of the society's particular struggle.[30] Yet such a view is somewhat unfair to the society's avowed insistence on a multi-faceted approach to societal issues. They established several "subject groups" – Political and Economic, Active Peace, Sexology, Philosophy and Religion, and The Arts – which met regularly and whose core concerns were worked into articles published in *Twentieth Century*. In its inaugural issue, Evans wrote that the journal would serve as a "vital co-ordinating bond of the many-sided work of the society, and will give expression to the results of that work."[31] A similar characterization of the journal would be expressed in a tipped-in circular appealing to new members in its eighth issue (October 1931). In fact, "A Challenge," as it was called, offers the most complete self-description of the Promethean Society available. Most significantly, the section "What We Stand For" lists four major

---

[30] G. Trease, *A Whiff of Burnt Boats* (London: Macmillan and Co. Ltd., 1971), pp. 132–3.

[31] J. R. Evans, "The Promethean Society: A Survey," *Twentieth Century* 1 (March 1931), p. 23.

positions: a rights-based planned economic life, world federation and disarmament, sexual rights and education, and a revamped child-centered education system.[32] The journal, then, as a kind of miscellany, could contain these multiple positions while presenting itself as singularly expressed and also serve as a vital communication link between all its members (who received a subscription to the journal upon joining). Yet, prior to the bookshop, there was no location advertised where one might purchase a copy – a reader had to either subscribe or write to Evans directly.

Despite such initial circulation restrictions, it is clear the journal reflected a vibrant and expansive organization. Across its thirty-five issues, from March 1931 to January 1935, *Twentieth Century* published content covering many interests and diverse, even contrasting, points of view. In the main, it contained poetry and prose by the likes of W. H. Auden, Naomi Mitchison, Stephen Spender, and George Barker; essays by Prometheans reflecting developments in their respective groups' meetings by Barraud, Pendle, Trease, Evans, among others; and some of the higher-profile contributors included Leon Trotsky, Havelock Ellis, Jose Ortega y Gasset, and Theodore Dreiser. The presence of so many recognizable names seems incongruous, especially as they might have possibly been unaware of the society's agenda. I believe the answer to this question comes in the form of

---

[32] "A Challenge," *Twentieth Century* 8 (October 1931). In the interests of a fuller representation of their positions on these issues, I quote the following from "What We Stand For": "[1] A rationally planned economic life based on the rights which every individual has as a member of society … [2] the recognition of the present existence of the world-community, for the surrender of national sovereignty to the interests of that community … [and] immediate and total disarmament … [3] the wide dissemination of knowledge of contraception, for the revision of the marriage and divorce laws and the laws relating to the unmarried mother, for inquiry and research into questions such as sterilization and abortion, for the building of a new sexual morality … [4] a complete restatement of educational theory … that morality and reasoning should arise from the child's actual experience and never of necessity from the authority or convenience of adults."

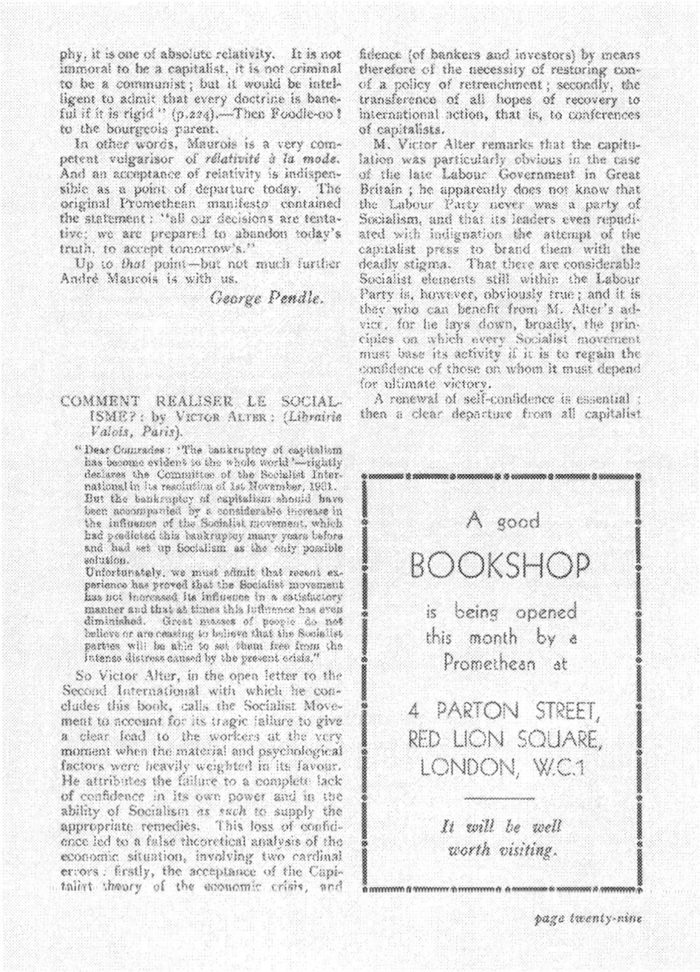

phy, it is one of absolute relativity. It is not immoral to be a capitalist, it is not criminal to be a communist; but it would be intelligent to admit that every doctrine is baneful if it is rigid " (p.224).—Then Foodle-oo ! to the bourgeois parent.

In other words, Maurois is a very competent vulgarisor of *rélativité à la mode*. And an acceptance of relativity is indispensible as a point of departure today. The original Promethean manifesto contained the statement : "all our decisions are tentative; we are prepared to abandon today's truth, to accept tomorrow's."

Up to *that* point—but not much further André Maurois is with us.

George Pendle.

COMMENT REALISER LE SOCIAL-ISME? : by VICTOR ALTER : (*Librairie Valois, Paris*).

" Dear Comrades : 'The bankruptcy of capitalism has become evident to the whole world '—rightly declares the Committee of the Socialist International in its resolution of 1st November, 1931. But the bankruptcy of capitalism should have been accompanied by a considerable increase in the influence of the Socialist movement, which had predicted this bankruptcy many years before and had set up Socialism as the only possible solution.

Unfortunately, we must admit that recent experience has proved that the Socialist movement has not increased its influence in a satisfactory manner and that at times this influence has even diminished. Great masses of people do not believe or are ceasing to believe that the Socialist parties will be able to set them free from the intense distress caused by the present crisis."

So Victor Alter, in the open letter to the Second International with which he concludes this book, calls the Socialist Movement to account for its tragic failure to give a clear lead to the workers at the very moment when the material and psychological factors were heavily weighted in its favour. He attributes the failure to a complete lack of confidence in its own power and in the ability of Socialism *as such* to supply the appropriate remedies. This loss of confidence led to a false theoretical analysis of the economic situation, involving two cardinal errors : firstly, the acceptance of the Capitalist theory of the economic crisis, and

fidence (of bankers and investors) by means therefore of the necessity of restoring confidence of a policy of retrenchment; secondly, the transference of all hopes of recovery to international action, that is, to conferences of capitalists.

M. Victor Alter remarks that the capitulation was particularly obvious in the case of the late Labour Government in Great Britain ; he apparently does not know that the Labour Party never was a party of Socialism, and that its leaders even repudiated with indignation the attempt of the capitalist press to brand them with the deadly stigma. That there are considerable Socialist elements still within the Labour Party is, however, obviously true ; and it is they who can benefit from M. Alter's advice, for he lays down, broadly, the principles on which every Socialist movement must base its activity if it is to regain the confidence of those on whom it must depend for ultimate victory.

A renewal of self-confidence is essential ; then a clear departure from all capitalist

A good

BOOKSHOP

is being opened
this month by a
Promethean at

4 PARTON STREET,
RED LION SQUARE,
LONDON, W.C.1

*It will be well
worth visiting.*

page twenty-nine

Figure 1 First advertisement for Archer's Bookshop, *Twentieth Century* (June 1932) (author's copy)

the journal's editor, and the person I argue most likely responsible for the idea of a Promethean Society bookshop, Jon Randell Evans.

Jon Randell Evans is one of the great overlooked figures of twentieth-century British publishing and letters. From the early days of Gollancz Ltd. in 1927, he served as one of the firm's key manuscript readers. Longtime Gollancz secretary Shelia Hodges claimed that "a very high proportion of the successes of the firm have been published on his recommendation."[33] The most notable example would be the approving report he wrote of John le Carré's first George Smiley novel *Call for the Dead* (1961), which effectively launched that author's publishing career.[34] Evans also authored two titles for Gollancz: a hastily compiled report entitled *The New Nazi Order in Poland* (1941) for the Left Book Club, which Evans acknowledged was mostly a compilation of data supplied by the Polish Ministries of Information and the Interior, and *The Junior Week-End Book* (1939), an activity book with a literary focus, of which Naomi Mitchison blurbed, "it's such a nice change from Hitler!" Even with his successes with the firm, Evans did not always have his way: for example, he failed to overcome Victor Gollancz's aversion to publishing poetry when recommending Auden.[35] It is a telling failure: Evans published Auden's "Get there if you can" in the first issue of *Twentieth Century* and took the trouble to thank the poet as one of those "who have helped in the difficult task of publishing this first number."[36] Indeed, the inclusion of names like Auden's or those of Ortega y Gasset, Trotsky, Dreiser, or Ellis seems less surprising if we consider the kind of access Evans would have to names and addresses as a reader at an increasingly popular publishing firm. And Evans certainly worked the system to his advantage: Promethean and later BBC nature presenter Desmond Hawkins usefully pointed out that Evans also went by "Hugh Macmillan, literary agent."[37] "Hugh Macmillan" only ever

---

[33] S. Hodges, *Gollancz: The Story of a Publishing House, 1928–1978* (London: Victor Gollancz Ltd., 1978), p. 63.

[34] A. Sisman, *John le Carré: A Biography* (New York: HarperCollins, 2015), p. 214.

[35] Hodges, *Gollancz*, p. 73.　[36] Evans, "The Promethean Society," 24.

[37] D. Hawkins, *When I Was: A Memoir of the Years between the Wars* (London: Macmillan London Ltd., 1989), p. 74.

advertised in *Twentieth Century*, beginning in the summer of 1932, at one address: 4 Parton Street.

Evans's strong handle on the publishing trade and the manner in which the shop was announced make it clear the bookshop was a Promethean venture from the start. On the heels of the Prometheans joining SPES in spring 1932 (Archer would join in October 1932), the society began advertising a "central distributing agency" for *Twentieth Century* at 4 Parton Street from its June 1932 issue, the same issue in which the bookshop was first announced:

> A good BOOKSHOP is being opened this month by a Promethean at 4 Parton Street, Red Lion Square, London, W.C.1. It will be well worth visiting.[38] (Figure 1)

The next month, the ad reads:

> Not last month but THIS month! ARCHER'S is opening! BOOKS 4 Parton Street, Red Lion Square, W.C.1.

The journal is tied to 4 Parton Street for the following twelve months, and the shop does not begin to advertise itself outside of the pages of *Twentieth*

---

[38] "Advertisement," *Twentieth Century* 16 (June 1932), p. 29. The first Hugh Macmillan ad, which ran in the same issue, reads: "HUGH MACMILLAN Authors' Agent BP+ We realize that in these days of economic and psychological depression a new Authors' Agency, if it hopes to be successful, must offer 'a little something others haven't got'. That is why, in the handling and placing of manuscripts, we are offering service which is the Best Possible – Plus. We suggest that you write to find out from us what that Plus is. We handle all types of manuscripts, and, of course, we only charge when manuscripts are placed. Our address is 4 Parton Street, Red Lion Square, W.C.1." ("Advertisement," *Twentieth Century* 16 [June 1932], p. 31). One presumes the reveal upon writing to Hugh what the "little something others haven't got" would have been a job approving manuscripts at a successful publishing firm. It begs the question how many of Hugh Macmillan's clients were sent to Gollancz for Jon Evans's manuscript approval resulting in a nice payment for Hugh Macmillan.

Century until the first issue of *New Verse* in January 1933. Whatever Archer's role was in establishing the bookshop beyond supplying the capital remains unclear. It is more than likely the idea for the shop was a society decision aimed at benefiting the circulation of the journal and, by extension, building visibility for the society itself. This leaves us with David Archer, the proprietor of the bookshop, whose personal life has been subject to much speculation and mythologizing, but who was clearly the personality who drove the identity of this establishment.

3 No.4 Parton Street

The business at 4 Parton Street offers a rich example of how a bookdealer and his stock gave a bookshop its identity. To appreciate how the shop came to define Parton Street as a literary scene, we need to first understand the motivations of it proprietor, David Archer. Retrieving the life of David Archer remains complex – he left nothing behind and the several accounts by friends muddles basic facts. But rather than trying to correct the entire record, I approach Archer on his own terms to argue that his early life and education pointed toward a career in social work, not bookselling. If we think of Archer as a kind of social worker for poets, then the form and function of the bookshop become clearer. This section moves from introducing Archer and his interests, to examining how his stock was shaped by the Promethean Society and smaller publishers, to portraying how the shop doubled as an organizational space for various activist causes, and finally to considering the life of the shop after Archer grew distant from its day-to-day activities. By approaching the bookshop through its bookdealer, stock, events, and operations, I present it as a system of meanings actively shaping the literary networks with which the shop came in contact.

David Archer Alderson was born to Marguerite and Captain (later Major) Samuel Frank Alderson April 15, 1907 in St. Peter Port, Guernsey (Figure 2).[39] In 1912, David's great uncle, another David Archer, died,

---

[39] *Census of the Islands, Guernsey, St. Peter Port* (1911), p. 39. The family lived several doors up the road from the house where Victor Hugo lived for many years and penned *Les Miserables* (1862), and the houses along Rue Hauteville

Figure 2 David Archer, 1950s (The John Deakin Archive/Bridgeman Images).

leaving his father a sizeable estate in Wiltshire. Samuel Frank Alderson added his uncle's surname "Archer" to his family's name by deed poll and relocated his family to oversee the business of the estate.[40] David would never have spent much time in Castle Eaton, where his father and mother lived for the remainder of their lives, but his father's business dealings with

command a stirring view of the harbor and its fortifications. "Hauteville House," www.maisonsvictorhugo.paris.fr/fr/musee-collections/visite-de-hauteville-house-guernesey [accessed March 10, 2019].

[40] "Samuel Frank Alderson Archer," *The London Gazette* (December 24, 1912), p. 9828. He reenlisted in late 1914 and served for the duration of the war on the Channel Islands, likely with his family in tow. After the war, David went to Kent House School in Eastbourne and from 1921, Wellington, a school that figures significantly later while he is managing his bookshop. See S. F. A. Archer, "Mein Kampf or My Adventures as Tenant for Life of the Castle Eaton Estate," Swindon, Wiltshire and Swindon History Centre, 2863.1 and "David Archer Alderson Archer," *Wellington College Register, 1859–1948*.

the family property, especially as they impacted his London literary activities has been subject to much speculation and rumor over the years.

And as with most rumor, the truth is less satisfying. In fact, despite dramatic tales of Samuel Frank Alderson Archer ruining himself selling off land to fund David's various projects, including the first printing of Dylan Thomas's *18 Poems*, the surviving property records do not tell a story of family ruin to indulge a spoiled child. In 1944, David's father typed out a seven-page memo describing the history of his inheritance and his property management. The memo is very detailed on the challenges, his solutions, and the available finances.[41] David may have been loose with his inheritance after his father's death in 1957, but the record of his father's estate management suggests that whatever financial contribution was made to establish the bookshop and publish titles under the imprint Parton Press in the 1930s was made within the

---

[41] Archer, "Mein Kampf," 2863.1. David's name only appears once and in the context of his father being unable to secure a mortgage as his son was underage at the time. What becomes clear in the memo is that Major Samuel Frank Alderson Archer was an attentive manager of his land holdings, even going back to school in 1912 to learn about estate management and farming at Cirencester Agricultural College; he was a conscientious caretaker of the money other family members (such as his mother and a close cousin) had tied up in the estate, and someone who was burdened by the Law of Property Act and other property, inheritance, and tax acts passed in 1925. Moreover, in the same year, he attempted to unload a bulk of the property he would now be legally required to upkeep at risk of penalty as its landlord and, for example, whose most appealing (and costly) holding – the Lushill House – had no well or running water. In short, the 1925 laws and the effort to sell off the land show that it did not matter when Major Archer sold his land, because the legal situation and its financial effects made it inevitable he would be obliged to do so during his lifetime. Ultimately, when David's father passed away in 1957, his estate was valued at more than £30,000, of which David inherited most of his monetary leavings, his car, and the contents of his house (more than £710,000 in 2018; "Bank of England Inflation Calculator," www.bankofengland.co.uk/monetary-policy/inflation/inflation-calculator [accessed April 18, 2019]). See "The Last Will and Testament of Samuel Frank Alderson Archer," District Probate Registry at Gloucester (February 11, 1957).

amount of an allowance to David outside of his father's business record. Simply, it never registered as a "cost" in his father's eyes or accounts.

David went up to Cambridge in 1925, examining in economics and psychology with a special subject in the British novel, earning his BA in 1928.[42] Most formatively, during his time at Cambridge, he co-founded the Marshall Society. Other founding members included Pat Sloan (joint secretary with Archer), Maurice Dobb (treasurer), and Philip Sargant Florence (president).[43] According to the society minutes, it aimed to "bring together members of the university and of the women's colleges who were interested in social questions; to increase an interest in such questions in the University and women's colleges; and to study these questions unbiased by Political or Religious prejudices."[44] During the time of Archer's involvement, from February 9, 1927, to the end of May 1928, the society hosted talks with a strong social welfare emphasis, took field trips to local villages and the social settlement Toynbee Hall in London, as well as hosting its warden J. J. Mallon and, most impactful for Archer, hosted the warden of Cambridge House, where he would later

---

[42] "David Archer Alderson Archer," Matriculation record for Gonville and Caius College, ref. /TUT/01/01/09. The special subject in the British novel seems like the most tantalizing detail of his university record, as it was taken immediately after E. M. Forster's 1927 Clark Lectures (later published as *Aspects of the Novel*). Forster, a fellow Kent House alum and fresh off publishing his class and inheritance tale *Howard's End*, may have had appeal for the son of a landowner faced with making his own way.

[43] Honorary vice presidents included John Maynard Keynes, Mary Paley Marshall, Goldsworthy Lowes-Dickinson, and A. C. Pijou, among others. Cambridge, Marshall Library of Economics, "Minutes of the Society," Marsoc1.

[44] "Minutes of the Society" (February 9, 1927), Marsoc1. T. E. B. Howarth cites promotional material I have been unable to track down, which asked: "Have you ever thought of taking an interest in the lives of other people? In all of us as a community? Of the boons of some and of the sorrows and difficulties of others? Oh, no, not a political society; nor a religious society – but a society unmoved by such prejudices." Quoted in T. E. B. Howarth, *Cambridge between the Wars* (London: William Collins Sons & Co. Ltd., 1978), pp. 150–1.

reside.[45] The minutes show David to be an active member: occasionally signing the minutes, being tasked with inviting guests, volunteering to coordinate the Industrial Welfare and Educational Group, joining the Arts Committee to help produce ads, putting his name to an unrealized plan to start a journal, and pitching the idea of organizing a boys' camp.

It is unclear what David did after leaving Cambridge, but the settlement house visits clearly influenced him, as by 1932 he was a resident at Cambridge House.[46] The Cambridge University settlements were one of three settlement initiatives – along with Oxford House and Toynbee Hall – created in the late nineteenth century to address the effects of mass poverty. Cambridge House in Camberwell, the central organizing location, was a "center where Cambridge men interested in their fellow-citizens could live, work, and obtain some knowledge of the conditions of life in South London."[47] The general idea of Cambridge House was that motivated Cambridge graduates could use their educational training in a social work context. During the time Archer resided there, Cambridge House ran "five clubs (three boys' clubs, two unemployed men's clubs), a Model Parliament, Care Committees, and a Poor Man's Lawyer."[48] During his time at Cambridge House he also joined the Protheans, whose education reform and broad appeal to youth drew Archer to Parton Street.

If Evans and the Protheans provided the impetus for the bookshop, Archer's capital funded it and, at least in the beginning, he was the face of the shop. I have been unable to establish who owned 4 Parton Street or what arrangement Archer made for the property; however, given that Archer's father made no mention of what would have been the costly purchase of a freehold in London, it is more than likely that Archer leased the building and rented out rooms to individuals and organizations (Figure 3). To give a sense of how Archer would have gone about renting the address and the

[45] "Minutes of the Society" (March 12, 1927; April 27, 1927), Marsoc1.
[46] *Electoral Register, Camberwell 1932* (London: Corporation of London Joint Archive Service), p. 16.
[47] *The History and Function of Cambridge House* (Cambridge: Bowes and Bowes, 1934), pp. 6–7. Full board was advertised at £2.10s.0d.
[48] *Cambridge House*, p. 19.

No. 4 Parton Street W.C.1   June 1959
                              AWG

Figure 3 No. 4 Parton Street (Camden Local Studies and Archives Centre).

costs involved, we have a contemporary example in Elkin Mathews booksellers. That business, needing to move to a more affordable location, hired an estates agent to locate a "Georgian house at a rent of £400 a year and were able to let out the top three floors at a profit."[49] The space at 4 Parton Street was comparable in size to that of Elkin Mathews.

> The building at 4 Parton Street was a small eighteenth-century house, only a corridor and a room wide and two rooms deep, consisting of a basement, ground, first, and second floors with our attic above. There was a sink off the stairs between the ground and the first floor and a lavatory in the tiny basement yard below.[50]

In addition to "Hugh Macmillan," and the parade of characters that will be discussed further along taking up residence at 4 Parton Street, there was the Communist Party of Great Britain (CPGB) co-founder T. A. Jackson (1934); scandal-prone Sidney Stanley (1934); the Film and Photo League (1935–6), an early version of the Artists' International Association (1935); and the final year of the Workers' Theatre Movement (1935), who all occupied the premises while Archer ran the bookshop. Vacancies were listed for multiple rooms in October 1935, and only Philip Poole seems to have rented an office at the address between 1936 and 1938 until Lawrence & Wishart installed Modern Books in an office later on (1939–40).[51]

---

[49] P. Bernard, "The Bookshops of London," in G. Mandelbrote (ed.), *Out of Print and Into Profit: A History of the Rare and Secondhand Book Trade in Britain in the 20th Century* (London: The British Library and Oak Knoll Press, 2006), p. 91. Charles Elkin Mathews published several important works throughout his life – *The Yellow Book* (1894), W. B. Yeats's *The Wind in the Reeds* (1899), James Joyce's *Chamber Music* (1907), and several early books of poetry by Ezra Pound. J. Wilhelm, *Ezra Pound in London and Paris 1908–1925* (University Park and London: Pennsylvania State University Press, 1990), pp. 5–6.

[50] B. Weinreb, "No. 4 Parton Street," *Camden History Review* 13 (1985), pp. 16–17.

[51] Sidney Stanley helped publish an issue of *Out of Bounds* and was arrested and fined for distributing the *Daily Worker* in 1934, shortly after he had published *That's Sedition – That Was! Being a Collection of Notable Sayings by the Prime Minister and*

The bookshop had modest visibility in its first twelve months; it advertised regularly in *Twentieth Century* until July 1933 and subsequently advertised in *New Verse*.[52] The *Twentieth Century*, even if its primary focus was not literary, attracted a key audience with its publishing of poetry and fiction, along with articles by Hugh Gordon Porteus, who was the Prometheans' Arts Group leader and a Wyndham Lewis devotee. He wrote on Lewis, Aldous Huxley, T. S. Eliot, T. E. Hulme, and a multi-part review of Bloomsbury for the journal.[53] *Twentieth Century* had also drawn the attention of Michael Roberts, who taught a few blocks from Parton Street at the Mercers' School, and who published *New Signatures* in 1932 for Hogarth Press. For that book, he culled from literary

---

Other Persons Above Criticism out of 4 Parton Street. He was later embroiled in an influence-peddling scandal, becoming a key figure investigated by the Lynskey Tribunal in 1949. For more on Stanley, including a 1933 deportation order and his ability to gain influence within political circles, see S. W. Baron, *The Contact Man: Sidney Stanley and the Lynskey Tribunal* (London: Secker & Warburg, 1966), pp. 62–3. See also "Heavy Sentences on *Daily Worker* Sellers," *Daily Worker* (August 8, 1934), p. 3. Raphael Samuel speculated that the rise of the Unity Theatre and the Left Book Club sped the demise of the Workers' Theatre Movement, as it gave leftists other creative and critical outlets outside of a theatre group that had been regularly critical of the Labour Left and had treated theater as "a splendid weapon of struggle … [while] reject[ing] what they called the 'theatre of illusion.'" R. Samuel, "Theatre and Socialism in Britain (1880–1935)" in R. Samuel, E. MacColl, and S. Cosgrove (eds.), *Theatre of the Left, 1880–1935: Workers' Theatre Movements in Britain and America* (London: Routledge and Kegan Paul, 1985), pp. 46, 58–64. Modern Books published "Comintern views on the war before the German invasion of the USSR." D. Cope, *Bibliography of the Communist Party of Great Britain* (London: Lawrence and Wishart Ltd., 2016), p.198.

[52] The advertising in *Twentieth Century* dropped when Evans moved the publication to a new address. It is somewhat unclear why this happened, but *Twentieth Century* changed its format by the end of the year, came out more irregularly, and published its final issue dated Winter 1934–5. It is outside the focus of this Element, but it appears that the Promethean Society was folded into the Federation of Progressive Societies and Individuals and its journal *PLAN*, which shared an address, printer, and layout design with *Twentieth Century*.

[53] For a detailed biography of Porteus, see J. Meyers, *Resurrections: Authors, Heroes – and a Spy* (Charlottesville: University of Virginia Press, 2018), pp. 59–73.

journals like *Criterion* and *Adelphi* and included three poets *Twentieth Century* had published – Auden, Stephen Spender, and A. S. J. Tessimond.[54] When John Middleton Murry, *Adelphi* editor and *Twentieth Century* contributor, tasked a fresh-faced George Barker with reviewing Roberts's *New Signatures*, Roberts repaid the favor by meeting with Barker and directing him to Archer's.[55] Barker's story proved to be an early instance of a Parton Street regular finding the bookshop by irregular means.

By the time *Twentieth Century* had moved its distribution from 4 Parton Street in summer 1933, the bookshop was attracting its own crowd. Some of this was a result of where and how Archer advertised the shop, including the regular emphasis on its lending library. Archer's advertised its stock for the poetry-centric *New Verse* as "Poetry Drama Criticism Marxist Literature and Periodicals Always in Stock" and announced it was "now arranging a small lending library of the more significant contemporary verse."[56] For the multi-focused *Twentieth Century*, it offered "a good selection of modern books and drama always on view," and its final advertisement noted that its lending library contained "[m]ost of the books recommended in the *Twentieth*

---

[54] J. Harding, *Criterion: Cultural Politics and Periodical Networks in Inter-War Britain* (Oxford: Oxford University Press, 2002), p. 160. Mercers' School was housed at Barnard's Inn Hall (Gresham College), about half-mile away in Holborn ("Gresham College: Mercers' School at Barnard's Inn," www.flickr.com/photos/greshamcollege/15183570176). Part of the exercise of this section is to reconstruct how the networks that formed through 4 Parton Street came to be, and proximity, as we will see, seems to have been a powerful and perhaps obvious, if overlooked, factor in this story.

[55] See J. M. Murry, "Notes on Communism," *Twentieth Century* 13 (March 1932), pp. 3–5, where Murry critiques communism in favor of a liberal individualism. Barker would have a lifelong, complicated friendship with Archer, monumentalizing him in 1973 with his poem *In Memory of David Archer*. For Barker's fateful meeting with Archer, see G. Barker, "Coming to London," in *Essays* (London: Macgibbon & Kee, 1970), pp. 68–69.

[56] "Advertisement," *New Verse* 2 (March 1933), p. 18. See issues 1,2, 3, and 6 of *New Verse* all in 1933. The ad copy in *Twentieth Century* changed to mirror the language in the *New Verse* ads around the same time.

Century."[57] Towards the end of 1934, the bookshop advertised in the first four issues of *Left Review* touting "left novels" and a "lending library of English and foreign books" costing five shillings a quarter featuring "*The Disinherited. In All Countries*. Wells' *Autobiography. Irreconcilables. Fontamara. A Hope for Poetry. Russian Sociology. Freedom and Organization*."[58] The advertisement shows a canny understanding of how to appeal to *Left Review* readers: the first three books listed and *Fontamara* were reviewed in *Left Review*, *A Hope for Poetry* was written by *Left Review* regular C. Day Lewis, and the Sidney Webb–prefaced *Russian Sociology* and Bertrand Russell's *Freedom and Organization* would have been of clear interest to the periodical's readership. The shop would have also been on the radar of *Daily Worker* readers from the outset. In the same issue announcing its opening, *Twentieth Century* published Maurice Dobb's "Marxism and the Crisis" and a letter from Dobb complaining that the journal had published Trotsky. The *Daily Worker* responded that the journal was indeed "anti-Marxist" for publishing Trotsky and expressed confusion over Dobb's decision to publish there.[59]

One might surmise that factional debates would have made good business for a bookshop supplying a wide variety of leftist material. For example, Esmond Romilly, Winston Churchill's nephew, left Archer's alma mater Wellington after immersing himself in Marxist literature and drawing the conclusion that public schools were deeply oppressive. His actions made national headlines and his (initially secret) arrival at 4 Parton Street gave the

---

[57] "Advertisement," *Twentieth Century* 19 (September 1932), p. 27. "Advertisement," *Twentieth Century* 31 (October 1933), back cover.

[58] "Advertisement," *Left Review* 3 (December 1934), inner front cover. See also issue 4 for the same ad copy.

[59] M. Dobb, "Marxism and the Crisis," *Twentieth Century* 16 (June 1932), pp. 1–5. M. Dobb, "Correspondence," *Twentieth Century* 16 (June 1932), p.24. "Dobb on Planning under Fascism: Wrong Article in Anti-Marxist Journal," *Daily Worker* (July 6, 1932), p. 4. The *Twentieth Century* had published Trotsky's "Communism and World Chaos" in two parts (the April and May 1932 numbers) with the qualifier that the journal "must not, of course, be taken as necessarily in agreement with the views expressed in the article" (6).

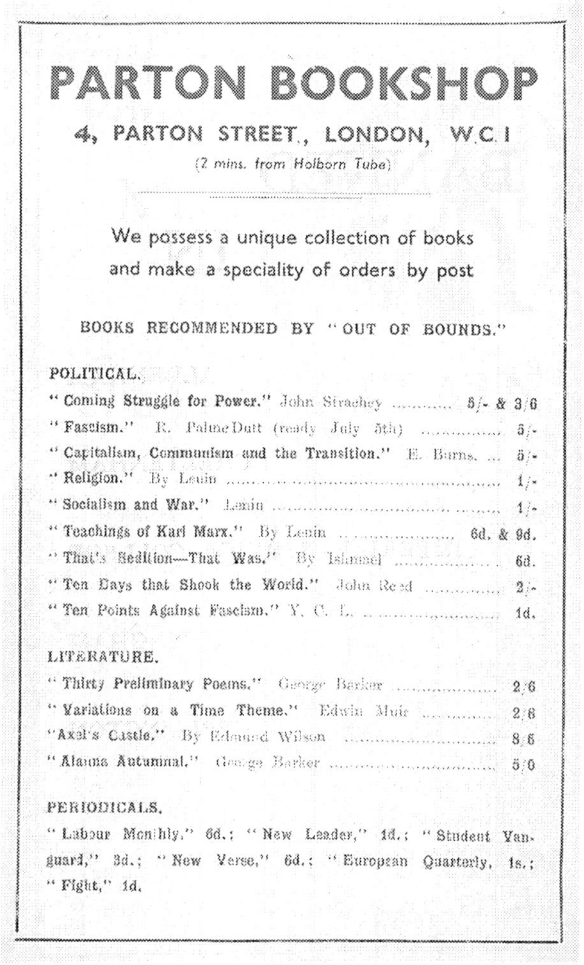

Figure 4 Parton Bookshop advertisements in *Out of Bounds* (British Library).

PARTON BOOKSHOP

4, PARTON STREET, LONDON, W.C.1

(2 mins. from Holborn Tube)

POLITICAL.

Coming Struggle for Power, John Strachey	5/- & 3/6
Fascism and Social Revolution, R. Palme Dutt	5/-
Lenin on Britain	8/6 & 5/-
Capitalism, Communism and the Transition, Emile Burns	5/-
The First Workers' Government, G. R. Mitchison	5/-
Guide to Modern Politics, G. D. H. Cole	6/-
History of Russian Revolution, Trotsky	10/6
Ten Days That Shook the World, John Reed	2/-
The Merchants of Death, Engelbrecht and Hanighan	7/6
The Soviet Theatre, P. A. Markov	5/-
Who Backs Mosley?	6d.

POETRY.

The Noise of History, John Lehmann	3/6
Poems, Stephen Spender	5/-
Poems, W. H. Auden	5/-
The Orators, W. H. Auden	7/6
Poems, T. S. Eliot	7/6

LITERARY.

Letters of D. H. Lawrence, edited by Aldous Huxley	8/6
Men Without Art, Wyndham Lewis	10/6
A Hope For Poetry, C. Day Lewis	6/-

NOVELS.

Shot Whilst Escaping, Schönstedt	7/6
Barricades in Berlin, Neukranz	2/-
Women Must Work, Richard Aldington	7/6
The Invaders, William Plomer	7/6

The Modern Schools Handbook	5/-
The Old School	7/6
The School, W. B. Curry	2/6
Science at the Cross Roads	5/-

PERIODICALS.

Labour Monthly, 6d.; Out Of Bounds, 1/-; Student Vanguard, 3d.; New Verse, 6d.; Cambridge Left, 6d.; This Unrest, 6d.; New Masses, 7½d.; Left Review, 6d.; Socialist Leaguer, 2d.; New Leader, 1d.

LENDING LIBRARY, 5/- A QUARTER.

Your Inspection is Invited.

We Make A Speciality of Orders By Post.

Figure 4 (cont.)

shop a new dimension.[60] He published the first three of four issues of his journal *Out of Bounds* from 4 Parton Street, worked at the shop, and tried his hand at political organizing all before he was sixteen, when, he co-wrote a memoir with his brother Giles in which they recounted the injustice of public schools and Esmond detailed his time at the bookshop.[61] *Out of Bounds*'s changing subtitles collectively describe its emphasis well: "Against Reaction in the Public Schools," "Public Schools' Journal Against Fascism, Militarism, and Reaction," and eventually "The Progressive Journal of the Public Schools." The journal, taken as a whole, is an interesting record of an engaged teenager's reading habits. Romilly appears to have had a hand in most of the content, and there are a surprising number of advertisements in so controversial a publication featuring publishers and bookshops, as well as numerous book and journal reviews (Figure 4). As a result of Romilly's energy and enthusiasm, we have the most detailed record of what the bookshop's stock looked like at any given moment.

If we take these lists as representative, while several publishers are reflected (sixteen in all excluding the periodicals), half of the stock comes from Victor Gollancz Ltd., Martin Lawrence, Wishart & Co., and Faber & Faber. From what we can glean from the advertising, Archer seems to have run his shop more along the lines of his larger competition (a mix of new and used with a lending library). This set the shop apart from other modernist bookshops like Harold Monro's Poetry Bookshop, which had more of a boutique premise, or Charles Lahr's Progressive Bookshop, which seems to have been run more like

[60] "Mr. *Churchill's* Nephew Vanishes from Public School: 'Under the Influence of London Communists,' Says Mother," *Daily Express* 10,532 (February 10, 1934), p. 1.

[61] There are several accounts of Esmond Romilly and *Out of Bounds*. See K. Ingram, *Rebel: The Short Life of Esmond Romilly* (London: Weidenfeld and Nicolson, 1985), pp. 50–86. P. Toynbee, *Friends Apart: A Memoir of Esmond Romilly & Jasper Ridley in the Thirties*, 2nd ed. (London: Sidgwick and Jackson, 1980), pp. 15–36. G. Romilly and E. Romilly, *Out of Bounds: The Education of Giles Romilly and Esmond Romilly* (London: Hamish Hamilton Ltd., 1935). Julian Symons curiously attaches an appendix to his *The Thirties: A Dream Revolved* listing public school denunciations of Esmond Romilly's *Out of Bounds* journal (the journal itself will be discussed later), especially as he only spares a paragraph mention of the brothers in his book complaining about the state of education then (pp. 38–9, 154–6).

a secondhand shop even if it stocked newer titles and by all accounts survived on his acquisitions acumen. Archer's also differed from these shops in that the Booksellers Association has no record of Archer's business, with whom he would have needed to register to get trade terms with publishers.[62] This effectively meant the bookshop existed outside of the formalized relations between publishers and booksellers. Archer would have had trouble finding trade terms, so he would have had to be creative in his acquisitions.[63] Certainly Evans would have helped with initiating a relationship with Victor Gollancz Ltd., and Martin Lawrence (33 Great James Street) and Wishart & Co. (9 John Street) were a few blocks away, leaving Faber & Faber, where one might speculate a connection through *Twentieth Century*. Archer's unusual approach to the book trade shows a bookseller invested in personal relationships and local networks over business concerns.

Archer's lending library represents another aspect of his trust in the local, but it was also a common service for a bookshop to offer. The shop's advertising regularly makes mention of a lending library, or more popularly referred to as a circulating library, and they were indeed a ubiquitous service in the 1930s. Circulating libraries date back to 1661; by the early twentieth-century, they were a common feature of the British book trade.[64] W. H. Smith's established

---

[62] T. Joy, *The Bookselling Business* (London: Pitman Publishing, 1974), p. 240. The Bookseller Association has no listing but admits it may be because the shop closed before it built its database (email from Pippa Halpin, BA membership manager, November 7, 2018). Even so Archer's is not listed in the 1933 *British Book Trade Directory*, which serves as a complete list of all Bookseller Association members.

[63] It is possible another overlooked figure of the trade played a role: the book traveler. Publishing firms would send travelers around to the shops to promote new releases and arrange sales. Given the close-knit publishing community represented by the firms named earlier, it is unlikely Archer strongly relied on the happenstance of a motivated book traveler coming round for the core of his stock, but it could explain how he was able to carry such a variety of imprints while not benefiting from Booksellers Association membership. For more on book travelers, see S. Unwin, *The Truth About Publishing* (London: George Allen and Unwin Ltd., 1926), pp. 164–75.

[64] J. Feather, *A History of British Publishing* (London: Routledge, 1988), p. 57.

libraries at railway stops; Boot's, the chemist's chain, founded the Booklover's Library in 1898 with the notion that the ailing bedridden read; Mudie's, which initially supplied Boot's, started its library in the mid-nineteenth century and dominated the trade into the 1930s; and the popular *The Times* Book Club had famously challenged the Net Book Agreement in its early years.[65] Circulating libraries were featured in many types of commercial ventures. Harrod's is one example, which in fact bought Mudie's stock when the latter went out of business in 1936.[66] Smaller bookdealers offered circulating libraries as a way to attract customers, even if the libraries themselves seldom generated much profit.[67] Archer's subscription rate of five shillings a quarter was comparable to the basic rates of the "Big Four" circulating libraries named earlier.[68] Circulating libraries remained controversial among publishers due to the perception they dropped sales, in addition to a certain snobbery in reaction to the Big Four's customer base.[69] Frank Swinnerton, who, like Evans, had been a

---

[65] Credit for Boot's Booklovers' Library goes to chain owner Jesse Boot's wife, Florence Boot. F. Sanders, *British Book Trade Organization: A Report on the Work of the Joint Committee* (London: George Allen & Unwin Ltd., 1939), pp. 135–6. F. Mumby and I. Norrie, *Publishing and Bookselling* (London: Jonathan Cape Ltd., 1974), pp. 230, 294).

[66] Mumby and Norrie, *Publishing and Bookselling*, p. 372.

[67] From a report submitted to the Publishers Association in 1928. Sanders, *British Book Trade Organization*, pp. 146–7.

[68] All four had a basic rate of around a pound a year and around 2 guineas for more exclusive access, such as newly published works. Sanders, *British Book Trade Organization*, pp. 138-9.

[69] George Orwell's "Bookshop Memories" generally takes a dim view of bookselling, but, expressing a graver concern the publishing houses, specifically sees lending libraries as invitations for theft: "How the book thieves must love those libraries! It is the easiest crime in the world to borrow a book at one shop for two pence, remove the label and sell it at another shop for a shilling. Nevertheless booksellers generally find that it pays them better to have a certain number of books stolen (we used to lose about a dozen a month) than to frighten customers away by demanding a deposit." G. Orwell, "Bookshop Memories," in P. Davison (ed.), *The Complete Works of George Orwell*, Vol. 10: *A Kind of Compulsion, 1903–1936* (London: Secker & Warburg, 2000), p.511. Orwell worked at Booklovers' Corner (October 1934–January 1936), run by

publisher's reader for many years, complained that the libraries' subscribers "roam around the shelves as if they did not know one book from another." The libraries themselves fare no better: "[s]helves and shelves; acres and acres of book-backs with unknown titles upon them, and unknown names."[70] Q. D. Leavis observed something similar in her visits to circulating libraries where customers submitted themselves to the clerks, arguing that "no one who has made a point of frequenting London and provincial branches of the book-clubs for the past few years can avoid concluding that the book-borrowing public has acquired the reading habit while somehow failing to exercise any critical intelligence about its reading."[71] For Archer, a circulating library would have been a practical business decision, but based on the evidence of the advertising, he also tailored it to a core customer base.

We know about Archer's stock from the shop's advertising, but tracking his sales is another matter. Unfortunately, no one writing about Archer's makes mention of how strong the shop's sales ever were.[72] Archer would have needed to do some regular business to keep the shop going. For

Independent Labour Party (ILP) members who were friends of his aunt. P. Davison (ed.), *Complete Works*, pp. 354–5. For Booklovers' Corner as raw material for *Keep the Aspidistra Flying*, see A. Thacker, "Circulating Literature," pp. 93–5.

[70] F. Swinnerton, *Authors and the Book Trade* (London: Gerald Howe Ltd., 1932), pp. 137–8.

[71] Q. D. Leavis, *Fiction and the Reading Public* (London: Pimlico, 2000), p.7. Leavis quotes Stanley Unwin, arguing that because circulating libraries are such a fixture in British life, a solution as to taste (which for Unwin translates into more of his authors selling) would be improved public education (Leavis, p. 9). She conveniently, for her own purposes, cuts off this long quote from Unwin before he admits that his complaint concerns availability in circulating libraries not the institution itself; he generally well regards its practitioners. See S. Unwin, *The Truth About Publishing*, pp. 176–8.

[72] The closest case involves Weinreb discussing packing up the stock to be sold off to Bertram Rota in 1939, including the remaining copies of *18 Poems*. Bertram Rota was unable to confirm what came of this transaction, and neither was Weinreb's former business partner. B. Weinreb, "No. 4 Parton Street," p. 18. Emails from Julian Rota (April 24, 2019) and Julia Elton (May 22, 2019).

example, a report submitted to the Publishers Association in 1935 painted a bleak financial picture for what is described as "Mr. Average Bookseller." For a business doing £17,606 in sales a year, the business could expect a net profit of just £71.[73] Trade terms at the time were highly variable, with 33 percent a general maximum with a so-called daily rate or a one-off order of 25 percent, and this report assumes an average 27 percent trade discount from publishers.[74] Thomas Joy, writing in 1952 after a couple of decades in the trade, quoted this report, asserting that "few shops can deal in *new books only*," adding that "[b]efore the war the selling of new books was not economically stable."[75] Joy observed that this report accounted for a mix of new and secondhand book sales, and that selling new books only would have resulted in a 4 percent loss. His own specimen balance sheet of a well-run shop in 1949, which in essence has managed to limit stock in relation to sales, still only garnered a net profit of £690 after £10,566 in sales. Such grim findings put a lie to Orwell's claim in 1936 that "[g]iven a good pitch and the right amount of capital, any educated person ought to be able to make a small secure living out of a bookshop."[76] In the 1930s, a bookshop could only survive as a commercial enterprise if someone with capital and the ability to make good business decisions was taking action, it could not necessarily provide the financial stability Orwell claimed.

Archer clearly had no great financial ambition. His shop served a social mission. Nowhere was this more evident than the shop's role in the Scottsboro Defense Committee. The bookshop became involved through Archer's friendship with the sons of Lascelles Abercrombie, especially David Abercrombie. We know only bits and pieces of his friendship with David Abercrombie: as we learn from the advertisements in the first two issues of *Left Review*, the shop was briefly known as "Parton Bookshop: Archer and Abercrombie"; Ben Weinreb wrote that he was hired by Abercrombie and Vicki Darragh after Archer seems to have given up running the shop regularly; tellingly, David Gascoyne remembered a

---

[73] Sanders, *British Book Trade Organization*, pp. 46–7.

[74] Sanders, *British Book Trade Organization*, p. 45.

[75] Thomas Joy, *Bookselling* (London: Sir Isaac Pitman & Sons, 1952), p.69.

[76] Orwell, "Bookshop Memories," p. 512.

party he once hosted that Abercrombie attended, adding that "David Archer of Parton Street must have been there."[77] Yet, in his unpublished memoir, Abercrombie makes no mention of Parton Street or Archer; in fact, records reveal very little of those years in London.[78] But Abercrombie was very much involved in the Scottsboro Defense Committee headquartered at 4 Parton Street for a time. The nine Scottsboro boys, falsely accused of the rape of two white women in 1931, had become an international cause thanks in no small part to Nancy Cunard, who was quite active around London in 1933 fund-raising for the legal defense in the ongoing court case.[79] The several iterations of the Scottsboro Defense Committee had different degrees of involvement by Cunard and other notable names like Naomi Mitchison, Vera Brittain, and Jomo Kenyatta.[80] The committee led by the Abercrombies – David served as secretary and Lascelles was the honorary treasurer – regularly posted announcements in *The Daily Worker*.[81] A pamphlet – "We Were Framed: The First Full Account Published in

[77] "Advertisement," *Left Review* 1 (October 1934), inside rear cover. "Advertisement," *Left Review* 2 (November 1934), inside rear cover. B. Weinreb, "No. 4 Parton Street: The History of a Left-Wing Bookshop," *Camden History Review* 13 (1985), p. 16. D. Gascoyne, *Collected Journals* (London: Skoob Books Pub Ltd., 1991), p. 348.

[78] An obituary mentions only that he was an assistant lecturer at the London School of Economics (1934–8). See J. Kelly, "David Abercrombie," *Phonetica* 50.1 (1993), pp. 66–9. The David Abercrombie papers are held at the Edinburgh University Centre for Research Collections but are, as of the date of this writing, unprocessed. Staff archivist Paul Fleming has kindly confirmed that the uncatalogued memoir does not mention either the bookshop or Archer (email from Paul Fleming, August 27, 2018).

[79] I. Gordon, *Nancy Cunard; Heiress, Muse, Political Idealist* (New York: Columbia University Press, 2009), p.200.

[80] S. Pennybacker, *From Scottsboro to Munich: Race and Political Culture in 1930s Britain* (Princeton: Princeton University Press, 2009), pp. 46–7.

[81] For example, see "London Scottsboro Appeal Committee," *The Daily Worker* (December 14, 1933), p. 4; "Scottsboro Boys Appeal," *The Daily Worker* (March 2, 1934), p. 1; "Advertisement for Left Theatre event in co-operation with the Scottsboro Defence Committee," *The Daily Worker* (June 30, 1934), p. 4; "The

England of the Trials of the Nine Scottsboro Boys" – was addressed at 4 Parton Street. David Abercrombie was clearly the point man for this initiative, using Archer's shop, much like the Promethean Society before him, as an organizational center.[82] As we have seen, from the Promethean Society to the Scottsboro cause, and all the briefly 4 Parton Street–stationed ventures in between, Archer treated the shop as a center for social causes akin to the Cambridge House. His involvement, though, extended beyond hosting.

Archer came to be a publisher as well, setting up the Parton Press imprint and publishing the first books of George Barker and Dylan Thomas, and the first non-self-published book by David Gascoyne, all under the imprint of Parton Press.[83] The common thread through these publications was that the three were regulars of the bookshop, with Thomas intermittently residing there in his early years in London. Because there was not much consistency in Archer's motivation to publish these three poets, or perhaps because he did not expand Parton Press into a fuller list of publications, credit for putting these books out has always been qualified.[84] But the details suggest something else at work: yes, Thomas roomed at 4 Parton Street with Ben Weinreb, but at various times so did Maurice Carpenter, Romilly, Toynbee, T. A. Jackson, and Winnie Barham. All

Scottsboro Defense Committee Presents Famous Negro Artistes in an All-Star Entertainment," *The Daily Worker* (May 23, 1935), p. 2.

[82] As a curious example of how clearly David Abercrombie was in charge, an MI5 intercept of a Comintern message to the Communist Party of Great Britain instructed an agent to "send by mail from address of a non-Communist 3 repeat 3 pounds to following address: DAVID ABERCROMBIE, c/o ARCHER'S Book Shop, PARTON Street, KINGSWAY, W.C.1 LONDON." N. West, *Mask: MI5's Penetration of the Communist Party of Great Britain* (London: Routledge, 2012), p. 133.

[83] He would later publish the first books of W. S. Graham and Dom Moraes.

[84] For more on how these poets came to be published by Archer, see R. Fraser, *Night Thoughts: The Surreal Life of the Poet David Gascoyne* (Oxford: Oxford University Press, 2012), p.96; R. Fraser, *The Chameleon Poet: A Life of George Barker* (London: Pimlico, 2014); A. Lycett, *Dylan Thomas: A New Life* (New York: The Overlook Press, 2004), pp. 103–4.

this support was repaid with a collective attitude that Archer had no business sense, and his open-heartedness with his friends was a financial liability. Whatever the validity of such insights into Archer, I believe there is a more constructive way to approach his actions and the particularly relaxed nature of the bookshop itself: first, the fact that he moved back to Cambridge House in 1935 when accounts of his presence on Parton Street are lacking (hence Weinreb's hiring),[85] and second, when he reappeared in Manchester in 1939, opened another bookshop, published Barker again, and listed himself as a "social worker" in a local Manchester register.[86] The return to Cambridge House and the later professional declaration show that Archer saw himself first and foremost as a social worker with the shop serving as a convenient means to help the young and marginalized. *Twentieth Century*, the Prometheans, *Out of Bounds*, the three books of poetry, the Scottsboro appeal, the bookshop and the rooms above were all social causes in need of a champion, or at least a home.

Other acts in Archer's life are outside the concerns of this book, but even if he had more or less removed himself from operating the shop by 1935, the shop itself remained a going concern at 4 Parton Street for years to follow. Ben Weinreb dated his arrival, and the gradual distancing of Archer from the shop, to the spring of 1935.[87] Weinreb was hired by Abercrombie and Vicki Darragh, who themselves had other businesses occupying their time.[88] In this moment, Winnie

---

[85] *Electoral Register, Camberwell 1935* (London: Corporation of London Joint Archive Service), p. 14. An October 1935 "Offices Vacant – To Let" advertisement in the *Daily Worker* lends credence to this theory that Archer had left the premises more or less for good (three rooms: a light room, a smaller room, and the basement). *Daily Worker* (October 21, 1935), p. 8.

[86] *England and Wales Register, Lancashire, Manchester 1939*. Archer published George Barker's *Elegy on Spain* (1939). For comment on his Manchester bookshop, see "A Good Risk," *Manchester Evening News* (April 21, 1939), p. 12.

[87] Weinreb, "No. 4 Parton Street," p. 15. Weinreb, like many others with Archer, has gotten basic facts wrong, asserting that Archer "failed to get a degree at Cambridge" (p. 15). As we have seen, he did earn his degree.

[88] Abercrombie was advancing his fledgling academic career, and Darragh was regularly writing for *The Daily Worker* in 1936 and 1937 about the wage crisis for

Barham took over the shop. Barham is an interesting puzzle: she is regularly referred to in memoirs as a name the reader should know, but she has no public visibility outside running the shop. She was listed as a masseuse addressed at 4 Parton Street specializing in medical gymnastics and medical electricity throughout the 1930s. During her years running the shop, she lived at Trease's old address at 1 Lamb's Conduit Street (1936) adjoining Red Lion Square, and at 37 Red Lion Square cohabiting with Archer's fellow Marshall Society founder Pat Sloan (1937–39).[89] Advertising in *Contemporary Poetry and Prose* and *Left Review* from May to August 1936 lists the Barham-run business now as "New Books" with a "cafe downstairs."[90] The shop at 4 Parton Street retained its stock and audience and still advertised Parton Press titles.[91] Its relationship to the newly formed Lawrence & Wishart, the Left Book Club, and Popular Front politics in general will be discussed

miners and other events. Darragh's first byline appear on January 8, 1936, in an interview with the president of the Miners' Federation of Great Britain, and her name appeared 53 times over the following two years.

[89] The *Chartered Society of Massage and Medical Gymnastics: Register of Masseuses and Masseurs* has listings for Barham at 4 Parton Street from 1934 to 1938. See also Electoral Register entries in Holborn for 1936–9.

[90] "New Books" advertised in all ten issues of *Contemporary Poetry and Prose*, see especially "Advertisement," *Contemporary Poetry and Prose* 1 (May 1936), p. 15; "Advertisement," *Contemporary Poetry and Prose* 3 (July 1936), p. 71. Ads in *Left Review* were intermittent: "Advertisement," *Left Review* 2.9 (June 1936), p. 480. "Advertisement," *Left Review* 2.11 (August 1936), p. 592. Another indication of the changes in late 1935–early 1936 comes in the form of the aforementioned October 21, 1935, rental ad in the *Daily Worker*: "OFFICES VACANT: LET. – LARGE LIGHT ROOM, suitable office; also smaller room and basement, cheap. Suitable store or workroom. – PARTON BOOKSHOP. 4. PARTON STREET, W.C.1." See also first ad after a gap in some months, "Advertisement," *Daily Worker* (June 3, 1936), p. 6.

[91] An advertisement in the ninth issue of *Contemporary Poetry and Prose* (March 1937) lists "New Books" as "Agents for Parton Press," suggesting a distinction between the shop and the press to the extent that Archer was no longer a part of 4 Parton Street by this date.

in the next section, but one small example from this time demonstrates how the shop had become a modernist institution beyond the intentions of its founder.

Contemporary Poetry and Prose, a journal produced by Roger Roughton out of 1 Parton Street, ran advertisements in the winter of 1936 for *New Directions in Prose and Poetry*, listing 4 Parton Street as "Agents for Great Britain." James Laughlin was just starting New Directions and his first publication just months earlier provides some insight as to how 4 Parton Street linked up with Laughlin. The first author Laughlin published, Wayne Andrews, introduced the New Directions publisher to Paul Eluard and Andre Breton, who themselves were published by *Contemporary Poetry and Prose* and who had attended the 1936 Surrealist Exhibition in London that summer.[92] While the actual details of this networking are obscure, it does show that, for a time, the bookshop was an important space in the networks of transnational literary modernism.

Roughton, who left the business of *Contemporary Poetry and Prose* with 4 Parton Street after the last issue, was one of many individuals who had passed through, found use, and in many ways came to define what 4 Parton Street was.[93] This is best reflected in the fact that the most familiar imaginings of the shop and David Archer come from memoirs and interviews of those who were there. Despite the presence of Darragh and Barham, and the possible links women like Mitchison and Cunard had to the shop, the accounts are almost all by men.[94] George Barker, Maurice Carpenter, John Cornford, David Gascoyne, Desmond Hawkins, John Heath-Stubbs, Esmond Romilly, Derek Stanford, Julian Symons, Philip

---

[92] For Laughlin's links to Eluard and Breton, see I. MacNiven, *Literchoor Is My Beat: A Life of James Laughlin* (New York: Farrar, Straus and Giroux, 2014), p.97.

[93] For the closing of the journal, see "Announcement," *Contemporary Poetry and Prose* 10 (Autumn 1937), p. 2.

[94] Rosalind Wade's account is a compilation of other (unattributed) sources; despite attempting to put the reader in the bookshop, as it were, she left it unclear whether she was ever at the shop (even if Maurice Carpenter places her there). See R. Wade, "The Parton Street Poets," *Poetry Review*, 54.4 (Winter 1963–4), pp. 290–7. Stephen Spender was interviewed for the Esmond Romilly biography and ungenerously remembers Archer as a "hopeless character." K. Ingram, *Rebel*, p. 51.

Toynbee, Geoffrey Trease, and Rosalind Wade all write about the shop and David Archer. Their works are filled with half-remembered events, assumptions about Archer and his family, and collectively operate as a portrait of a gossipy milieu that must have fueled so much of the activity in that shop. Barker is a wonderful example – dismissive of so much of Archer's choices, he wrote a long poem memorializing his friend after Archer's death:

> What a bore all those politically affiliated young men
> at your Parton Street Bookshop were, David, in those
> forgettable thirties. They resembled waiters
> bringing one a sort of cold vichysoise Utopia
> on a tin tray, and they resented violently the perversity
> that makes one turn away from such a degrading dish
>
> …
>
> Why on earth go to the trouble
> of setting the stars in their heavenly operations
> and the planets in their circles of serenity
> simply in order to decorate a picnic
> held by the Engineers' Union?[95]

The tension that runs throughout the poem involves Barker's issues with his own feelings about the scene he was wrapped up in the 1930s and his affection for Archer, who is inextricable from that complicated past. But unpacking the different versions of everyone's memories or, indeed, attempting to validate or question Barker's critique clouds the fact that the bookshop was a charged space for many who passed through its doors.

One scene, told from three different perspectives, will close out this section and it is hoped provide some sense of what the bookshop meant for those who

---

[95] G. Barker, *In Memory of David Archer* (London: Faber and Faber, 1973), p. 36. As to the partial nature of Barker's memory, 4 Parton Street hosted a "surprise social" for the Weddell Bros (posters) strikers in the summer of 1935. See "Advertisement," *Daily Worker* (July 23, 1935), p. 4; "Advertisement," *Daily Worker* (July 26, 1935), p. 4.

frequented it. The following are Maurice Carpenter's, Esmond Romilly's, and Philip Toynbee's memories of Toynbee arriving at 4 Parton Street for the first time having been inspired by Romilly to run away from school:

CARPENTER: Philip Toynbee arrived from Rugby, a tall, willowy youth. The electricity in the shop was cut off – a crisis we were always expecting, and we groped about in the dark for candles and electric torches.

ROMILLY: [A] boy of about seventeen came round to our office and asked if I were in. He had followed my example and 'run away,' although this time it was Rugby which had been found unpopular as a permanent residence. I had never met him before, and we had only corresponded once or twice, so I thought it a little optimistic on his part to come to London with myself as his only means of finding accommodation. Still, as he pointed out cheerfully when I told him this, there was always the Embankment.

Our 'house-party' was made merrier at the same time by the electric light being cut off. We had often managed without the gas or telephone, but this was a new adventure. I mention this to show that it was always rather an odd household.

TOYNBEE: [Upon meeting Esmond and entering the shop] That shop! The archetype of all the 'People's Books', 'Workers' Bookshops', 'Popular Books' that I was to know so intimately in the next five years. The solemn red-backed classics of the Marx-Engels-Lenin Institute, the mauve and bright yellow pamphlets by Pollitt and Palme Dutt, the Soviet posters of moonlit Yalta and sunlit tractors – the whole marvelous atmosphere of conspiracy and purpose ... Now [Esmond's] welcome was as warm as I could wish, and, sitting in the closed bookshop under a fierce bust of Lenin, I became voluble and boastful.[96]

[96] Carpenter, *Rebel in the Thirties*, p. 61; Romilly, *Out of Bounds*, pp. 286–7; Toynbee, *Friends Apart*, pp. 18–19.

This scene of three outcasts plotting to take over the world by candlelight in a closed bookshop neatly illustrates, to borrow Gilbert Fabes on Foyle's, the "romance of a bookshop."[97] Yet, as Toynbee's account implies, there was an entire network of radical publishing and bookselling beyond the walls of 4 Parton Street, in fact, from April 1936, just on the other side of the wall, as Lawrence & Wishart opened its doors for the first time.

4 No.2 Parton Street

By the time Lawrence & Wishart (L&W) arrived on Parton Street in 1936, the literary community associated with that street had been active for some time. There is no record of why the publishers chose this address, but their arrival fit comfortably with the scene as it existed. L&W's physical proximity to Archer's had symbolic importance, but the publisher's connections with radical booksellers like Archer's presents an opportunity to explore the nature and significance of the publisher-bookdealer relationship.

L&W formed in January 1936 and opened at 2 Parton Street that April. As the articles of association indicate, "Martin Lawrence and Wishart Ltd." formed through the joining of Martin Lawrence and Wishart & Co. Martin Lawrence had been the CPGB's publisher since 1925 and the amalgamation with Wishart & Co., whose three key figures – Ernest Wishart, Douglas Garman, and Edgell Rickword – were members of the Communist Party (CP), signaled a stronger commitment to publishing more radical literature.[98] It is important to note both their party affiliation and their

---

[97] G. Fabes, *The Romance of a Bookshop* (London: Privately printed, 1938).

[98] C. Hobday, *Edgell Rickword: A Poet at War* (Manchester: Carcanet Press Ltd., 1989), pp. 168–9. D. Cope, *Central Books: A Brief History 1939 to 1999* (London: Central Books Ltd., 1999), p. 15. While a full treatment of the history of Lawrence and Wishart's early years is still to be written, its stock was certainly more varied and literary minded before the merger. For example, arguably its most enduringly popular publication from the 1930s – Nancy Cunard's *Negro Anthology* (1934) – which was released as "Published by Nancy Cunard at Wishart & Co." with an assist from Rickword, was carried by Lawrence and Wishart for years afterward with languishing sales. C. Hobday, *Edgell Rickword*, p. 149. The correspondence for the remainder of the decade concerned how to

relative autonomy in publishing decisions: while L&W was most definitely CP aligned, it was not a CP publishing house. That being said, its alignment brought it into close coordination with the CP's retail arm in Britain – the Workers' Bookshop and CP-member-run Collet's Bookshop – and increasingly so throughout 1937 and 1938. This party alignment also brought L&W into cooperation with Victor Gollancz Ltd. and the Left Book Club (LBC), a club that had originated as an idea at the Workers' Bookshop (itself Gollancz's main distributor in the mid-1930s).[99] The publishers, book club, and bookshops, taken together, formed a briefly strong publishing identity for the CP in Britain c. 1936–9.[100]

L&W's early identity was also defined by 4 Parton Street. When L&W moved to 2 Parton Street, it brought the *Left Review* with it (Rickword was editor of both the press and journal at the time), but it did not consider opening a storefront.[101] However, Central Books, a kind of successor to

move the more than 500 copies in sheets with a cheaper binding and L&W eventually being able to bind 100 late in 1939. New Haven, Beinecke Rare Book and Manuscript Library, Yale University, GEN MSS 703 Box 2 fol. Nancy Cunard (1937–9). The book, published in February 1934, sold 241 copies that year, 33 in 1935, and 6 through April 1936 before the merger. New Haven, Beinecke Rare Book and Manuscript Library, Yale University, GEN MSS 703 Box 7 fol. Record of book sales 1934–6. Christopher Hilliard, focusing on what he calls "worker-writers," emphasized how uneven the publisher was with its treatment of its supposedly politically aligned authors and would-be authors. See C. Hilliard, *To Exercise Our Talents: The Democratization of Writing in Britain* (Cambridge, MA: Harvard University Press, 2006), pp. 134–6.

[99] R. D. Edwards, *Victor Gollancz: A Biography* (London: Victor Gollancz Ltd., 1987), p.227. The contract for the Left Book Club was subsequently shifted to Collet's. D. Cope, *Central Books*, p. 11.

[100] As Dave Cope's exhaustive *Bibliography of the Communist Party of Great Britain* (2016) makes clear, the CPGB had no shortage of outlets for publishing material, but the party's membership always remained low. Yet, the network I will outline in this section reached a much broader audience mostly due to the rapid success of the Left Book Club.

[101] The floor plan for 2 Parton Street was thus: Basement – Store; Ground floor – Dispatch counter, telephone, waiting room; First floor – Manager, Sales, Typist;

Figure 5 Still from *Escape Route* showing books for sale outside Central Books and the absence of 1 Parton Street across the way, 1950s (Renown Ltd.).

the Workers' Bookshop, which took over 2 Parton Street after 1939, chose to open a ground-floor shop that can be spotted in a few frames of the 1952 film *Escape Route* (Figure 5). It is possible that, with 4 Parton Street next door, L&W saw its neighbor as a kind of proxy storefront. This would explain both how Ben Weinreb could claim that L&W was "our main source of supply and the only publisher to allow us limited credit" and why

Second Floor – Board room, Editorial, Bookkeeper; Third Floor – *Left Review*, Left publishing, 2 flats. New Haven, Beinecke Rare Book and Manuscript Library, Yale University, GEN MSS 703 Box 7 fol. Meetings of Directors.

4 Parton Street appears nowhere in the surviving L&W financial documents of that period.[102]

Two bookshops that do appear prominently in L&W's financial records were Collet's Bookshop and the Workers' Bookshop.[103] Around the same time, L&W began offering a 33 percent discount off their titles to LBC members and published a "cheap edition" of *New Writing* 1 (already published by Hogarth Press) in the LBC signature orange cover with black type. L&W's efforts to reach out to a broadly left audience in 1936–7 reflected the Communist International's memorandum on forming a Popular Front of European political and cultural organizations. The publisher's retraction into more orthodox CP fare in 1938–9 was in some ways informed by the Moscow trials and also the complicating financial situation of having embraced the LBC so

---

[102] B. Weinreb, "No. 4 Parton Street," *Camden History Review* 13 (1985), p. 18. An undated CPGB "Memorandum on Literature" broke down the "historical machinery" of CP literature distribution, which included "[s]hops run by sympathizers with their own finance, but with extended credits, and which can be brought in to any new scheme." New Haven, Beinecke Rare Book and Manuscript Library, Yale University, GEN MSS 703 Box 7 fol. Financial position 1938–9. In essence, what Weinreb noted about credit was a matter of CP policy, and 4 Parton Street did advertise its name change to "New Books" in 1936 in *Left Review*. When L&W had the idea to publish Communist International (CI) material again (something Martin Lawrence did before), it reopened "Modern Books" and set it up in a room next door (advertised as "4a Parton Street"). For a brief history of Modern Books, see D. Cope, *Bibliography of the Communist Party of Great Britain* (London: Lawrence and Wishart, 2016), pp. 198–9. For L&W's decisions regarding Modern Books, see New Haven, Beinecke Rare Book and Manuscript Library, Yale University, GEN MSS 703 Box 6 fol. Figures 1936–9. The May to August numbers of *Left Review* and *Contemporary Poetry and Prose* show the "Parton Bookshop" becoming "New Books" by June 1936, and "reopening" a cafe at 4 Parton Street by August 1936. See especially advertisements in *Contemporary Poetry and Prose* 1–4 and *Left Review* 2.11–13.

[103] They were the only two bookshops individually itemized in the spreadsheets with the remaining shops listed simply as "Others."

wholeheartedly.[104] In this transition, Collet's and the Workers' Bookshop became more central to L&W's plans, so it is worth examining how these bookshops did business – both with their customer base and the CP-aligned L&W.

Collet's Bookshop was opened in 1934 at 66 Charing Cross Road as "the political bookshop – an independent bookshop dealing in all advanced publications" at the former site of Henderson's "The Bomb Shop."[105] It was co-founded by Eva Collet Reckitt (who gave the shop its name) and Olive Parsons and included Maurice Dobb as one of the first members of its board. Despite the business not being greatly profitable, it had shops in Glasgow, Manchester, and Cardiff by 1937.[106] Like Archer's, it advertised itself as a dealer in leftist literature: "Call in some time and see our supply of working-class books"; "Keep to the LEFT / All the literature of the LEFT movement / Traveling Library of LEFT Books / Tickets for all LEFT Functions / Spring List of all LEFT Books and Pamphlets on application. Join the Left Book Club at Collet's."[107] It served as the headquarters for the

---

[104] For the CI's role in the Popular Front, see M. Worley, *Labour Inside the Gate: A History of the British Labour Party between the Wars* (London: I. B. Tauris & Co. Ltd., 2008), pp. 207–16.

[105] "Advertisement," *Daily Worker* (January 17, 1934), p. 4.

[106] "The shop opened with a manager and an assistant, with Eva and Olive Parsons both helping out. The 'Bomb Shop' had cost £617; made up of £167 to take over the lease. And £450 to settle the accumulated debts to publishers. Weekly takings during the first six months of trading averaged £38 15s 4d, and the net loss over this first period was £194 1s 0d. Christmas week 1934, however, saw a net profit of just over £9, and the same week there took place the opening of Collet's Glasgow Bookshop. This was followed by a Manchester Bookshop in April." J. Saville, "Eva Collet Reckitt: Communist Bookseller," in J. M. Bellamy and J. Saville (eds.), *Dictionary of Labour Biography*, Vol. 9 (Houndmills: Macmillan, 1993), pp. 240–1. The Cardiff shop opened in October 1936. D. Cope, "Radical Bookshop History Project," Left on the Shelf Books: Research Pages, p. 30. www.leftontheshelfbooks.co.uk/images/doc/Radical-Bookshops-Listing.pdf

[107] "Advertisement," *Daily Worker* (February 24, 1934), p. 4. "Advertisement," *Left Review* 2.9 (June 1936), p. 478.

Figure 6 2 Parton Street as Central Books, 1950s (Camden Local Studies and Archives Centre)

Writers' International, the outfit that originally produced the *Left Review*, the first five issues of which were addressed at 66 Charing Cross Road. The Writers' International, founded after a meeting in February 1934 at Conway Hall as an organization of writers desirous of ending "the capitalist order of society … together with the working-class journalists and writers who are trying to express the feelings of their class."[108] But more programmatically than Archer's, Collet's embraced the political activity organized at its address: in particular, *The Road to '37* exhibition, which featured "books, posters, cartoons showing the struggle of six generations of workers for Peace Freedom and Democracy organized by Collet's Bookshops (under the personal direction of G.D.H. Cole)."[109] Yet, even with the bookshop's clear commitment to the cause, Collet's managed to straddle the worlds of CP publishing/organizing and more general interest bookselling in such a way that it was never really under the thumb of the CPGB or subject to its oscillating fortunes. The situation with its counterpart of sorts, Workers' Bookshop, was quite different.

Since its inception in 1920, the CPGB had some form of retail arm through which it could circulate its literature. Originally the Communist Bookshop, later renamed Workers' Bookshop, the business opened at CPGB head-quarters at 16 King Street in 1921 and later moved to Marx House at 38 Clerkenwell Green in 1927 and then to 49 Farringdon Road in 1937, and ultimately closed in 1939 to be replaced by Central Books (Figure 6). The Workers' Bookshop released a monthly bulletin promoting featured stock and would irregularly put out books and pamphlets itself – the most notable being a coproduced edition with Collet's Bookshop of Upton Sinclair's *No Pasaran! (They Shall Not Pass) A Story of the Battle of Madrid* (1937).[110] In

---

[108] "Writers' International (British Section)," *Left Review* 1.1 (October 1934), p. 38. Curiously, there is no record of this event having taken place in the *Ethical Record*.

[109] Indeed, as Cole reveals in the introduction, most of the exhibition consisted of his personal collection of material. *The Road to '37: An Exhibition* (London: Collet's Bookshops, 1937), pp. 5, 6.

[110] D. Cope, *Central Books*, pp. 9–13. The Communist Bookshop was raided by MI5 in 1925, prompting the CPGB to change the name to something not so on brand,

essence, the CP had differing forms of involvement in various institutions, a fact it attempted to get a handle on by 1939 with the establishment of Central Books as the main publisher, distributor, and retailer of party material in the UK. A 1939 memorandum argued for a more centralized plan for its distribution and described the CPGB's network of bookshops and distribution centers at that time:

(a) The Workers Bookshop which does (i) wholesale work, (ii) retail work, finances (iii) agents and (iv) shops, as well as being (v) the central depot for the L.B.C.
(b) Collets Shops. London, Glasgow, Manchester, and Cardiff. In the last three places they act as the District distributing center.
(c) Shops under Districts, but which are in reality financed by The Workers Bookshop.
(d) Shops run by sympathizers with their own finance, but with extended credits, and which can be brought in to any new scheme.
(e) Agents in Party Branches, Trade Unions, Labour Parties, etc.
(f) Newsagents and wholesalers who are handling our stuff direct from the Workers' Bookshop.[111]

To review: L&W had absorbed the CP's publishing arm in Britain and housed *Left Review*, which had originated at Collet's, a bookshop that had formed through some CP networking by way of the Workers' Bookshop. It is the nature of these close relationships that gave most of these establishments their relative autonomy from the CP and kept them open to a broader range of leftist publishing. It also made this network seemingly ideal for Victor Gollancz's Left Book Club.

Gollancz launched the Left Book Club in early 1936 in an effort to bring together Labour Party politicians and CP members to combat the worrying advances of fascist powers in Europe. He enlisted John Strachey and Harold Laski as co-selectors for titles and launched the seminal series in May 1936

as well as separating the bookshop's financial structure from the Party's. E. Cocaign, "The Left's Bibliophilia in Interwar Britain: Assessing Booksellers' Role in the Battle of Ideas," *Twentieth Century Communism* 4 (2012), p. 224.
[111] GEN MSS 703 Box 7 fol. Financial position 1938–9.

with Maurice Thorez's *France Today and the People's Front*. Neither the general idea of a book club nor the specific idea for the Left Book Club originated with Victor Gollancz. He responded to a suggestion made by Worker's Bookshop staffer Charlie Hall for such a club at a luncheon with John Strachey and Sir Stafford Cripps.[112] The Left Book Club, while associated with leftist politicians of various stripes and the Popular Front, was not formally associated with any political or social organization. Rather, it sought to create the space in which ideas and policies could be explained, analyzed, and debated – primarily, but not limited to, issues of war, poverty, and socialist reform.[113] Subscribers paid for six months, receiving a book a month and a copy of *Left News* – the latter printed information on the book selections and editorials and served an organizational function, printing information on Left Book Club meetings and events.

Early twentieth-century book clubs in Great Britain presented challenges to publishers and booksellers. As we have seen, *The Times* Book Club ran afoul of the Publishers Association in 1905 in what was perceived as a violation of the NBA, but *The Times* Book Club worked more like a circulating library with an option to buy recently published but previously circulated or "used" titles for below net price.[114] The book clubs that began cropping up in the 1930s tended to have a theme and sold new titles that, in cases like the Left Book Club, were specifically produced for the club. The affordability of book club rates had broad appeal, but were treated with suspicion by bookdealers for several reasons: (1) claims they would reduce prices generally reducing turnover (2) or encroach on booksellers' existing customer base; (3) the fear of "direct trading," or mailing titles to subscribers eliminating the bookdealer as a go-between; and (4) concerns they circumvented the NBA, and by extension, gave the impression that

---

[112] D. Cope, *Central* Books, p. 11. J. Lucas, *The Left Book Club: An Historical Record* (London: Victor Gollancz Ltd., 1970), p.15.

[113] J. Lucas, *The Left Book Club*, p. 26.

[114] R. J. Taraporevala, *Competition and Its Control in the British Book Trade, 1850–1939* (London: Pitman Publishing, 1973), pp. 75–6.

other titles were overpriced.[115] These fears were often unfounded, as Margaret Cole has argued:

> [T]he Left Book Club, even where it publishes new books, is not in competition with the ordinary trade. It sells through ordinary bookshops, but its selling strength does not lie there so much as in the "left" political bookshops to whose growth it has made so great a contribution. The second point is that, to the great majority of those who have joined it and to those who do propaganda for it, membership of the Left Book Club is a political act, a social duty, a contribution to a good cause.[116]

When book clubs had a political or religious focus, membership was strong, but not overwhelmingly so, and certainly not to the extent that it would be ruinous for booksellers. Cole collected membership numbers for several book clubs of the time, including the seven that W&G Foyle Ltd. ran, and they indicate focused interests if not the giant numbers circulating libraries like Boots could brag about.[117] Whatever the actual impact on the trade, book clubs had achieved enough of a market presence by 1939 for the Publishers Association and the Association of Booksellers of Great Britain and Ireland to step in and attempt to regulate them. In its joint statement, "Regulations for the Conduct of Book Clubs," all book clubs needed to be registered, a title could only be published as a book club edition after twelve months from its first release, and it forbid "direct trading only" membership

---

[115] Taraporevala, *Competition and Its Control*, pp. 174–8.

[116] M. Cole, *Books and the People* (London: The Hogarth Press, 1938), p. 28.

[117] Cole, *Books and the People*, pp. 21–7. Taraporevala, *Competition and Its Control*, pp. 173–4. In fact, Foyle's the bookseller cashing in on the book club phenomenon showed how much room there was in the market for multiple niche interests – the seven it ran included the Right Book Club (25,000 members), "The" Book Club (26,000 members), Religious Book Club (6,000 members), Travel Book Club (5,000 members), Catholic Book Club (5,000 members), Scientific Book Club (5,000 members).

setups so that booksellers could have an opportunity to carry the book club editions.[118] Political and religious book clubs were exempted from these regulations.[119] Gollancz, who had always signed the NBA unwillingly, had a contentious relationship with the Publishers Association, hating what he perceived to be restrictive trade practices, once shouting "I refuse to be manacled by fools."[120] Gollancz's rebarbative spirit may have put him at odds with regulatory bodies, but it was clearly part and parcel of his publishing decisions.

And in the case of the Left Book Club, he had made a decision that, as it quickly gained traction, the book trade could not ignore. The Left Book Club grew its initial membership by advertising in leftist newspapers where interested subscribers were initially directed to Victor Gollancz Ltd.'s address, then Collet's and the Workers' Bookshop.[121] L&W, seeing a market it could capitalize on, joined the bandwagon. In July 1937, the Left Book Club announced that all L&W titles were available "at two-thirds of the ordinary price" to all Left Book Club members.[122] The advertisement clearly shows Gollancz's motivation for the partnership – namely, in forming alliances across the Left: "When it is remembered that L&W publish (in addition to many other important books) a large range of Marx-Engels & Lenin classics the importance of this new development can hardly be over-estimated."[123] And L&W's motivation can be illustrated by

---

[118] F. Sanders, *British Book Trade Organization: A Report on the Work of the Joint Committee* (London: George Allen & Unwin Ltd., 1939), pp. 178–86.

[119] Readers of political and religious books were perceived to be niche audiences who did not frequent libraries or bookshops; in the case of political content, it was generally believed it dated too quickly to create real competition problems. Taraporevala, *Competition and Its Control*, p. 175.

[120] R. D. Edwards, *Victor Gollancz: A Biography* (London: Victor Gollancz Ltd., 1987), pp. 169, 384–5.

[121] "Left Book Club [advertisement]," *New Statesmen and Nation* (February 29, 1936), pp. 124–5. "Advertisement," *Daily Worker* (May 1, 1936), p. 7. "Advertisement," *Daily Worker* (May 2, 1936), p. 6. "Left Book Club Enrollment Form," *Daily Worker* (May 27, 1936), p. 3.

[122] "Advertisement," *Daily Worker* (July 10, 1937), p. 5.

[123] "Advertisement," *Daily Worker* (July 10, 1937), p. 5.

the Left Book Club subscriber numbers – 18,000 by September 1936 and more than 50,000 by 1938. Joseph Gordon Macleod, author of the great modernist poem *The Ecliptic*, also has the distinction of being the first to organize a Left Book Club Group. The bookshop at 4 Parton Street also joined in advertising as "Agents for the Left Book Club." It could later be found hosting at least one Left Book Club meeting for *Secret Agent of Japan* by Amleto Vespa.[124] The Left Book Club was quickly a success and had reached all corners of radical bookselling in Britain in a very short amount of time.

The partnership between the Left Book Club and L&W was strong in the beginning as well, with the two organizations collaborating to publish *Modern Quarterly*, a scientific journal with a "conviction that the pursuit and application of scientific knowledge in the modern world cannot be isolated from the social relations in which they are carried on."[125] Yet, by the end of 1938, it was clear the partnership had not generated any benefits for L&W. For example, in the first two months of the partnership (August-September 1937), L&W sold 929 titles to Left Book Club members out of a total 56,197 copies sold, and only 1,351 to Left Book Club members in the last three months of 1938 as a

---

[124] "Central London Youth Group. On November 17th at 7:30 at New Books, 4 Parton Street, W.C.1, there will be a discussion on *Secret Agent of Japan*." "Left Book Club [advertisement]," *Left Review* 2.12 (September 1936), p. 658. Membership shot up to 44,800 after twelve months and then plateaued at around 53,000 by the end of 1938. Lewis, *Left Book Club*, p. 33. Cole, *Books and the People*, p. 39. Lewis, *Left Book Club*, p. 14. Also, 4 Parton Street joined in advertising as "Agents for the Left Book Club." "Advertisement," *Daily Worker* (June 3, 1936), p. 6. *Left News* 31 (November 1938), p. 1065.

[125] "Editorial," *Modern Quarterly* 1.2 (March 1938), p. 103. In its "Statement of Aims" in its opening number, the editors established that the journal would "contribute to this realistic, social evaluation of the arts and sciences ... [and further] the periodical will devote special attention to studies based upon the materialistic interpretation of the Universe, and to the mutual relations between intellectual activity and the social background." "Statement of Aims," *Modern Quarterly* 1.1 (January 1938), p. 3. The editorial board included such LBC authors as J. D. Bernal, J. B. S. Haldane, Laski, H. Levy, and Joseph Needham.

similar percentage of the total.[126] A report on the Left Book Club scheme spells out L&W's hope to tap into the 50,000 strong Left Book Club membership; however, after implementing it for more than a year, L&W noticed no rise in sales and worried about the costs involved due to lack of turnover.[127] By the end of 1938, the L&W board had voted to end its association with the Left Book Club and simplify its publishing plan for 1939.

Present at that meeting were representatives for Collet's and the Workers' Bookshop who, while not officially a part of the L&W structure, were informally integrated into L&W's publishing plans by 1938. One way to approach the reason would be all the ways in which the CP was involved in their various businesses, but another equally valid explanation would be the numbers. The Workers' Bookshop and Collet's accounted for 59 percent of L&W's sales between April 1936 and July 1937, or between L&W's instantiation and the start of the Left Book Club scheme. Even if the percentage trended downward from 69 percent in 1936 to 45 percent in 1937, these two bookshops were the main distributors of L&W stock for some years.[128] Simply put, the Workers' Bookshop and Collet's were L&W's

---

[126] New Haven, Beinecke Rare Book and Manuscript Library, Yale University, GEN MSS 703 Box 6 fol. Figures 1937–8.

[127] They also reference booksellers' complaints about the scheme; while they are careful to note these include bookshops "unconnected to the firm or the Movement," presumably the lackluster sales were hitting Collet's and Workers' harder than other shops: "There is a great deal of evidence that the scheme is disliked by booksellers in general, and that it has had the effect of keeping our books almost entirely out of the bourgeois. The bookseller is not prepared to stock L.W. titles at full price, knowing that the members of the L.B. C. can obtain them under the scheme and that to a great extent non-members are also obtaining them through friends." There was an unwillingness to unplug from such a large potential customer base, but it is clear L&W desired to move on from the idea. New Haven, Beinecke Rare Book and Manuscript Library, Yale University, GEN MSS 703 Box 7 fol. Left Book Club Scheme 1938–9.

[128] The percentage drop from 1936 to 1937 can mostly be explained by the massive success of the 1936 *Spain Pictorial*, which sold 71,000 copies in the two bookshops in the first month alone (Workers' Bookshop – 59,000, Collet's – 12,000),

storefronts in the 1930s and the Left Book Club a partnership whose fate mirrored that of the Popular Front.

While it is not the purpose of this book to re-litigate the naiveté of many British CP members in the wake of the Moscow trials, it had a very real business impact on L&W, and by extension on the Parton Street scene in general. The most concise way to portray this story would be through the frame of Edgell Rickword's time with the publisher. Rickword had made his mark in the 1920s with his influential journal *The Calendar of Modern Letters* (1925–7), with its incisive "Scrutinies," or takedowns of bloated literary reputations like that of J. M. Barrie or Walter de la Mare. He had moved on from the journal to form Wishart & Co. with fellow *Calendar* editors Cecil Rickword and Douglas Garman, along with Garman's monied brother-in-law Ernest Wishart.[129] Wishart & Co.'s publication record was stronger in literature than politics before the merger, with Rickword as an exacting editor – seeing the value of assisting Nancy Cunard in the final stages of compiling and printing *The Negro Anthology*, but by way of his cousin and business partner Cecil also rejecting Basil Bunting's translation proposal for a French biography of Rimbaud.[130] The merger with Martin Lawrence would have been agreed to by CP member Rickword, who was also on the board of Wishart & Co., but when it became clear L&W would publish the party line on the trial, along with the press's general back turning on literature titles, he stepped away from both *Left Review* and L&W in the summer of 1937.[131] As the example of Rickword illustrates, the hardening of

or almost a fourth of the total L&W sales for the year. As for the lasting relationship, Workers' Bookshop replacement Central Books and Collet's accounted for 39 percent of L&W total sales in the second quarter of 1941. GEN MSS 703 Box 6 fol. Figures 1936–9.

[129] Hobday, *Edgell Rickword*, pp. 107–8.

[130] New Haven, Beinecke Rare Book and Manuscript Library, Yale University, GEN MSS 703 box 1 fol. Basil Bunting.

[131] Hobday, *Edgell Rickword*, pp. 185–8. He remained a committed Marxist throughout his life, and he never strayed far from this network of publishers and booksellers, accepting a job at Collet's in 1957, working for the bookshop chain for nine years (mostly in its rare books department at its Charing Cross Road address). Hobday, *Edgell Rickword*, pp. 254, 259, 270.

party lines, the effects of the Spanish Civil War on British artists and writers, and the fickleness of "scenes" all meant that by 1939 Parton Street had ceased to be a thriving center of literary and political networking.

5 No.1 Parton Street and Beyond

Not much of Parton Street survived World War II – 2 Parton Street and 4 Parton Street suffered bomb damage, and even as Central Books carried on at 2 Parton Street into the 1950s, postwar urban planning saw fit to eventually build over the road completely. All of 1 Parton Street, including Meg's Cafe, was leveled early in the Blitz. I close with a look at Meg's for two reasons: first, if Archer's was what drew people to Parton Street, then the cafe was where they lingered – it gave the street its capacity to be a scene; second, its obliteration serves as the absent reminder of the limits of the archive in telling the tale of modernist institutions (Figure 7).[132]

Everyone came to Meg's Cafe. In addition to everyone named earlier, Charles Madge, Stephen Spender, Kathleen Raine, George Reavey, and even T. E. Lawrence were spotted at the cafe. Meg's was importantly where Roughton published *Contemporary Poetry and Prose* while living above the cafe. It was arguably the only sustained Surrealist periodical of interwar Britain.[133] It published Surrealists in translation, the Parton Press poets, and featured advertisements for New Books and Parton Press in every issue. When Roughton ended the periodical's run in September 1937, he announced that "[a]ny enquiries, or any orders for back numbers … should be sent to New Books, 4 Parton Street, W.C.1."[134] *Contemporary Poetry and*

---

[132] Esmond Romilly described Meg's as an "offshoot of the bookshop, as people who came into it always went to 'have coffee' across the road." Romilly and Romilly, Out of Bounds, p. 241.

[133] See M. Chambers, *Modernism, Periodicals, and Cultural Poetics* (London: Palgrave Macmillan, 2015), pp. 55–76. R. Mengham, "Nationalist Papers Please Reprint" in P. Brooker and A. Thacker (eds.), *The Oxford Critical and Cultural History of Modernist Magazines*, Vol. 1: *Britain and Ireland, 1880–1950* (New York: Oxford University Press, 2009), pp. 688–703.

[134] "Announcement," *Contemporary Poetry and Prose* 10 (Autumn 1937), p. 2.

Figure 7 Parton Street and Southampton Row, 1934 (London Metropolitan Archive)

Prose advertised "The Arts Cafe" at 1 Parton Street in its first issue, and the cafe's name change was perhaps an attempt to capitalize on the identity of the scene.[135] Philip J. Poole, who ran a stationery company at 4 Parton Street, also organized several rambling clubs and at least one meeting at Meg's. Rambling clubs had grown very popular by the 1930s ever since Leslie Stephen formed the first one in 1879, and many of the clubs had clear social or political interests.[136] Poole wrote about and advertised in the *Daily Worker*, and the aforementioned Meg's meeting saw a jointly organized ramble by the London Labour Sports Association and the Liberty Rambling

[135] "Advertisement," *Contemporary Poetry and Prose* 1 (May 1936), p. 15.
[136] M. Jebb, *Walkers* (London: Constable and Company Ltd., 1986), pp. 154–6.

Club.[137] Nor were Poole's rambling clubs the only ones to announce meetings at Meg's. The Federation of Progressive Societies and Individuals, a kind of successor to the Promethean Society, used Meg's as one of its addresses for meetings: J. B. Coates formed its Economics Discussion Group there (March 19, 1935), and the Education Group met there to discuss a proposal on primary education (April 9, 1935; May 13, 1935). Perhaps most endearingly, just before fifteen-year-old Esmond Romilly ran away, during a trip to London, he organized a lunch meeting at Meg's with his mother, David Archer, and CP members to persuade his mother of the justness of his cause in pursuing *Out of Bounds*. According to Romilly, his mother was briefly charmed by the idea.[138]

As for the other point Meg's illustrates: when it comes to the archive and modernist bookshops, there are depressingly few surviving collections. Huw Osborne's book unintentionally highlights this fact – it features only bookshops with some form of extant archival record. Archives like the Harry Ransom Center (The University of Texas at Austin) and the Archive of British Publishing and Printing (University of Reading) are wonderful resources for modernist print culture research, including records pertaining to bookshops. There are also recovery projects, such as Dave Cope's meticulous detailing of CP publications and booksellers in Britain, especially his history of Central Books. But far more common are stories like Archer's, who gave up control of the shop at some point in the 1930s and, according to Weinreb, the remaining stock, including the Parton Press, was sold to Bertram Rota booksellers. Archer lived a peripatetic life, attempting a few more shops and a couple more publications with the Parton Press (first books by W. S. Graham and Dom Moraes), before ending his own life in 1971. His effects were shipped to his extended family

---

[137] P. J. Poole, "Sunday Ramble," *Daily Worker* (May 14, 1936), p. 6.

[138] See Romilly, *Out of Bounds*, pp. 240–3. Esmond had a somewhat unique perspective on Archer, whom he dubs "David Bowman" and a "pillar of respectability" in the memoir. It is somewhat outside the focus of this Element, but from Romilly's reports, Archer was in regular touch with Esmond's mother and seemed willing to encourage his activities while attempting to regulate them. See Romilly, *Out of Bounds*, pp. 250–61.

in Castle Eaton, including his ashes secured in a desk drawer, and it remains a puzzle who precisely might possess those effects, if indeed they survived at all. It is not a story unique to David Archer. Boris du Chroustchoff, owner of the Salamander Bookshop, went out of business in the 1930s but kept his remaining stock. This stock was sold off over the years to places like Blackwell's in Oxford to support the family, but little of the history of the business remains outside of some catalogues and a Nina Hamnett sketch of the bookshop in the family's possession.[139]

What such examples show us is that the archive of the modernist bookshop primarily survives in the personal accounts and effects of its patrons and owners, which is perhaps fitting. Future research into such institutions needs to be sensitive to the heterogeneity and non-collectedness of their material archive. There is also a greater need for research that considers modernism and the book trade. Osborne's book, the recent *Publishing Modernist Fiction and Poetry* edited by Lise Jaillant, and the new volume *The Cambridge History of the Book in Britain*, Vol. VII: *The Twentieth Century and Beyond*, all clearly demonstrate the growing awareness of the importance of analyzing the trade that put modernism into print. I chose to focus on a single bookshop partly to foreground the component parts of this modernist institution but also to present how great an effect a single bookshop can have in a literary community. But as the other bookshops mentioned in this Element illustrate, future study of the trade in London alone might consider an abundance of shops and their communities.

Charles Lahr's Progressive Bookshop has appealed to a few scholars as of late.[140] Lahr revived Henderson's *Coterie* as *New Coterie* (1925–7), did much to help distribute an edition of D. H. Lawrence's *Lady Chatterley's Lover* and *Pansies*, published the controversial James Hanley novel *The German Prisoner* (1930), hosted Nancy Cunard while she was compiling *The Negro Anthology* (1934), and befriended C. L. R. James, providing James with his early reading on Marxism and

---

[139] Email from Natasha de Chroustchoff (April 5, 2019).

[140] Lahr has been the subject of three recent, careful considerations by Hilliard (2012), Osborne (2015), and Thacker (2019).

the Russian Revolution.[141] Lahr's bookshop, according to Thacker by way of Jean-Luc Nancy, "functioned as 'spaces of all kinds of opening' ... as a place for a developing community of ideas."[142] Thacker demonstrates this way of functioning not only with the examples identified earlier but by also situating Lahr's shop within the orbit of the more historically visible Parton Street community.

Archer's shop and Parton Street are also often referred to as the successor to Harold Monro's Poetry Bookshop.[143] Monro is best known within modernist studies for publishing Ezra Pound's *Des Imagistes: An Anthology* (1914) and Edward Marsh's series of Georgian poetry anthologies (1912–22), as well as founding and editing *Poetry Review* (1912–35). Bartholomew Brinkman, quoting Monro acknowledging the commercial benefits of a periodical ("we shall recommend the public what to read: in the Bookshop we shall sell them what we have recommended"), notes that "the Poetry Bookshop did not only promote various books and schools of poetry in its critical reviews but

[141] C. Høgsberg, *C.L.R. James in Imperial Britain* (Durham: Duke University Press, 2014), pp. 74–5. A. Thacker, "Circulating Literature: Libraries, Bookshops, and Book Clubs," in B. Kohlmann and M. Taunton (eds.), *A History of 1930s British Literature* (Cambridge: Cambridge University Press, 2019), pp. 89–104. H. Osborne, "Counter-Space in Charles Lahr's Progressive Bookshop," in H. Osborne (ed.), *The Rise of the Modernist Bookshop: Books and the Commerce of Culture in the Twentieth Century* (Farnham: Ashgate Publishing Ltd., 2015), pp. 148–9. Both Thacker and Osborne note C. L. R. James's claim that Lahr and his shop were vital to his "intellectual formation in the 1930s." See especially Osborne, "Counter-Space," p. 135. James may have also been familiar with Archer's. Louise Cripps, who had a relationship with James at that time, also claims to have co-founded *Twentieth Century* with Jon Randell Evans (even though she gets some of the key facts wrong). Evans was central to opening the shop at 4 Parton Street. L. Cripps, *C.L.R. James: Memories and Commentaries* (New York: Cornwall Books, 1997), pp. 115–6.

[142] Thacker, "Circulating Literature," p. 89.

[143] Although this was largely based on happenstance (Monro passed away a few months before Archer's opened its doors, and the Poetry Bookshop carried on until 1935).

also, in providing examples from poets and playwrights whose volumes could be found in the shop, they became metonymic of the Poetry Bookshop itself."[144] According to Brinkman, the "material juxtapositions" of the publications on the shelf mixed with the in-shop conversations, lectures, and readings can provide a fuller sense of modernism in the making.[145] In this sense, the Poetry Bookshop was also an example of how location mattered. Opened in January 1913 at 35 Devonshire Street, directly across Theobald's Row from Red Lion Square, where Monro believed its proximity to the British Museum was important as "people interested in literature were more likely to be found in the neighborhood of the British Museum than the West End."[146] Indeed, he was not alone in thinking so, as by 1934 at least forty-one bookshops were within two blocks of the British Museum, including eleven facing the museum on Great Russell Street. The Poetry Bookshop was one of those eleven after 1926 when its lease ran out at its first address, and Monro moved the shop to the back of 38 behind the retail address for George Routledge & Sons Ltd.–controlled publishers Kegan Paul, Trench, Trubner, & Co. Ltd., where it remained until 1935.[147]

Charing Cross Road rivaled the British Museum in numbers of shops, several with strong literary publishing credentials (Figure 8). The following fourteen bookshops were along a small stretch: E. Joseph (48A), Charles Jackson (50), International Book Shop (52), Henry Danielson (64), Henderson's (66), William Jackson (Books) Ltd. (68), Frederick B. Neumayer (70), Panzetta & Co. (72), Cyril William Beaumont (75),

---

[144] B. Brinkman, "'A Place Known to the World as Devonshire Street': Modernism, Commercialism, and the Poetry Bookshop," in H. Osborne (ed.), *The Rise of the Modernist Bookshop: Books and the Commerce of Culture in the Twentieth Century* (Farnham: Ashgate Publishing Ltd., 2015), pp. 123–4.

[145] Brinkman, "A Place Known," pp. 114–15.

[146] J. Grant, *Harold Monro and the Poetry Bookshop* (London: Routledge and Kegan Paul, 1967), p.61.

[147] Grant, *Harold Monro*, p. 164. *The British Book Trade Directory 1933* (London: J. Whitaker & Sons, Ltd.), pp. 168, 174.

Figure 8 Charing Cross Road, 1930 (London Metropolitan Archives)

P.J. & A.E. Dobell (77), Zwemmer's Bookshop (76 & 78), Joseph Poole & Co. (86), Miller & Gill (1924) Ltd. (94), and Foyle's (119–125 Charing Cross Road).[148] Add the dozen or so more on side streets like Cecil Court Road, and the "greater" Charing Cross Road area held near thirty shops.

Henderson's and *Coterie* were discussed earlier, but other shops like Beaumont's across the road deserve more attention. Beaumont's specialized in ballet books but also developed connections in the London literary community, especially with the Sitwells and Richard

---

[148] The locations of all the booksellers mentioned in this Element can be found on the *Layers of London* website. I will be regularly adding locations to the "Early 20th Century Bookshops" collection accessible here: www.layersoflondon.org/ map/collections/354

Aldington. Owner Cyril Beaumont ran The Beaumont Press out of the shop's basement.[149] It was a thriving press that published exquisite books with decorative boards, notably Walter de la Mare's *The Sunken Garden* (1917), W. H. Davies's *Raptures* (1918), Joseph Conrad's *One Day More* (1919), Richard Aldington's *Images of War* (1919, illustrated by Paul Nash), and D. H. Lawrence's *Bay* (1919).[150]

Zwemmer's, which regularly advertised in *New Verse* and was fondly remembered by Geoffrey Grigson, primarily sold high-end art books but also did trade in foreign language books.[151] Grigson described Zwemmer's as "all that the rest of London was not ... [it] was where we bought *Cahiers d'Art* ... discovered copies of *Blast* and *The Enemy* ... [it] was the one shop where the new and lively poetry and fiction were always in stock."[152] Founder Anton Zwemmer quit a stock job at Harrod's handling foreign correspondence and working the book section to apprentice at Richard Jaschke's at 78 Charing Cross Road in 1916 to eventually break out on his own purchasing Jaschke's Charing Cross Road shop in 1923.[153] By the 1930s, Zwemmer had opened Zwemmer's Gallery and expanded into 76 Charing Cross

---

[149] N. V. Halliday, *More Than a Bookshop: Zwemmer's and Art in the 20th Century* (London: Philip Wilson Publishers Ltd., 1991), pp. 26–7.

[150] For more on the Beaumont Press, see C. Beaumont, *Bookseller at the Ballet: Memoirs 1891 to 1929, Incorporating the Diaghilev Ballet in London, A Record of Bookselling, Ballet Going, Publishing, and Writing* (London: C. W. Beaumont, 1975), pp. 190–5. Aldington comes and goes throughout the memoir, but for the Sitwells, see especially pp. 142–5.

[151] F. Mumby and I. Norrie, *Publishing and Bookselling* (London: Jonathan Cape Ltd., 1974), pp. 362–3.

[152] G. Grigson, *Recollections: Mainly of Artists and Writers* (London: Chatto & Windus, 1984), p.39. The interactions between Zwemmer's and Archer's are suggestive. When Maurice Carpenter first met Archer, David took him over to Zwemmer's Gallery to see a friend's exhibition and have dinner at the Nanking Restaurant on Denmark Street (which regularly advertised in the *Daily Worker*). M. Carpenter, *A Rebel in the Thirties* (Wivenhoe: Paperbag Book Club, 1976), pp. 22–5.

[153] Halliday, *More Than a Bookshop*, pp. 22–3, 28–9, 33–5.

Road with a general literature shop. He also branched into publishing: notably, in the 1930s with Roger and Dylan Thomas, a special section Fry's *Henri-Matisse* (1930), Eugenio d'Ors's *Pablo Picasso* (1930) and *Paul Cezanne* (1934), and Herbert Read's *Henry Moore: Sculptor, An Appreciation* (1934).[154] Zwemmer's was also the book dealer for the International Surrealist Exhibition.[155]

Other bookshops in operation and part of this network of publishing, selling, and promoting included William Jackson (Books) Ltd., which had locations on Charing Cross Road and just a short ways southeast from Red Lion Square at Tooks Court, which specialized in foreign trade, particularly in North America. Co-director Alan Steele was responsible for having D. H. Lawrence's *Pansies* and James Joyce's *Ulysses* ordered from Sylvia Beach to be shipped to North America and attempted to get London shops to carry Gertrude Stein's *Tender Buttons*.[156] There was also W. J. Bryce, at 41 Museum Street, who had financial ties to George Allen & Unwin Ltd., thanks to the intervention of one-time Publishers Association president Stanley Unwin.[157] Salamander Bookshop, one of the many active antiquarian bookshops, was located between Red Lion Square and the British Museum on Silver Street. Owner Boris de Chroustchoff, who trained at Davis & Orioli, counted Nina Hamnett and Vaslav Nijinsky as customers and networked with people like William

---

[154] Halliday, *More Than a Bookshop*, pp. 281–2.

[155] The exhibition involved several Parton Street figures – not least Parton Press authors David Gascyone and Dylan Thomas, a special section in response in *Left Review* – and was a clear impetus for Roger Roughton's *Contemporary Poetry and Prose* – but it was Zwemmer's, not Archer's, which was invited to set up a bookstall at the New Burlington Gallery during the exhibition. Most likely, Zwemmer's was preferred on the strength of its foreign distribution contacts and contemporary fine art selections. Zwemmer's Gallery hosted several Surrealist shows throughout the 1930s. Halliday, *More Than a Bookshop*, pp. 152–3, 156–7, 303–6.

[156] Mumby and Norrie, *Publishing and Bookselling*, pp. 370–1.

[157] Mumby and Norrie, *Publishing and Bookselling*, pp. 376–7.

Empson and D. H. Lawrence.[158] Daughter Natasha de Chroustchoff maintains a Flickr page dedicated to her father, which stands as a living reminder of this bygone era of bookselling.[159] The lives, sales, and networks these bookshops represent serve as an impressive reminder of the breadth and depth of modernist literary production. More thought and attention to modernist bookshops would surely bring to light the granular details of this vital and vibrant institution.

[158] Email from Natasha de Chroustchoff (April 5, 2019). See also Chroustchoff at Davis and Orioli, www.flickr.com/photos/61377317@N05/sets/72157677157441603/ [accessed March 26, 2019].

[159] See www.flickr.com/photos/61377317@N05/albums/72157677157441603/

Archival Collections

Beinecke Rare Book and Manuscript Library, Yale University
Marshall Library Archives, University of Cambridge
Marx Memorial Library, London
Centre for Research Collections, The University of Edinburgh
People's History Museum, Manchester
Camden Local Studies and Archives Centre, London

References

"Advertisement," *Twentieth Century*, 16 (June 1932), 29.
"Advertisement," *Twentieth Century*, 19 (September 1932), p.27.
"Advertisement," *New Verse*, 2 (March 1933), p. 18.
"Advertisement," *Twentieth Century*, 31 (October 1933), n.p.
"Advertisement," *Daily Worker* (January 17, 1934), p. 4.
"Advertisement," *Daily Worker* (February 24, 1934), p. 4.
"Advertisement," *Left Review*, 1 (October 1934), n.p.
"Advertisement," *Left Review*, 2 (November 1934), n.p.
"Advertisement," *Left Review*, 3 (December 1934), n.p.
"Advertisement," *Daily Worker* (July 23, 1935), p. 4.
"Advertisement," *Daily Worker* (July 26, 1935), p. 4.
"Advertisement," *Contemporary Poetry and Prose*, 1 (May 1936), p. 15.
"Advertisement," *Daily Worker* (May 1, 1936), p.7.
"Advertisement," *Daily Worker* (May 2, 1936), p.6.
"Advertisement," *Left Review* 2.9 (June 1936), p.478.
"Advertisement," *Left Review*, 2.9 (June 1936), p. 480.
"Advertisement," *Daily Worker* (June 3, 1936), p.6.
"Advertisement," *Contemporary Poetry and Prose*, 3 (July 1936), p.71.
"Advertisement," *Left Review*, 2.11 (August 1936), p.592.

"Advertisement," *Contemporary Poetry and Prose*, 9 (March 1937), n.p.

"Advertisement," *Daily Worker* (July 10, 1937), p.5.

"Advertisement for Left Theatre event in co-operation with the Scottsboro" Defence Committee," *Daily Worker* (June 30, 1934), p. 4.

"Advertisement: Offices Vacant – To Let," *Daily Worker* (October 21, 1935), p.8.

"Announcement," *Contemporary Poetry and Prose*, 10 (Autumn 1937), p.2.

Archer, S.F.A. "Mein Kampf or My Adventures as Tenant for Life of the Castle Eaton Estate," Swindon, Wiltshire and Swindon History Centre, 2863.1.

Barker, G. "Coming to London," in *Essays* (London: Macgibbon & Kee, 1970), pp.67–73.

In Memory of David Archer (London: Faber and Faber, 1973).

Barker, N. "Obituary: Ben Weinreb," *The Independent* (April 7, 1999), www.independent.co.uk/arts-entertainment/obituary-ben-weinreb-1085605.html

Barnes, J. *Free Trade in Books: A Study of the London Book Trade since 1800* (Oxford: Clarendon Press, 1964).

Baron, S.W. *The Contact Man: Sidney Stanley and the Lynskey Tribunal* (London: Secker & Warburg, 1966).

Barraud, E.M. "The Revolt of Youth," *Everyman*, 3.63 (April 10, 1930), p.336.

Beaumont, C. *Bookseller at the Ballet: Memoirs 1891 to 1929, Incorporating the Diaghilev Ballet in London, A Record of Bookselling, Ballet Going Publishing, and Writing* (London: C.W. Beaumont, 1975).

Bernard, P. "The Bookshops of London," in G. Mandelbrote (ed.), *Out of Print and Into Profit: A History of the Rare and Secondhand Book Trade in Britain in the 20th Century* (London: The British Library and Oak Knoll Press, 2006).

Blair, S. "Local Modernity, Global Modernism: Bloomsbury and the Places of the Literary," *ELH* 71.3 (Fall 2004), pp. 813–38.

Braddock, J. *Collecting as Modernist Practice* (Baltimore: Johns Hopkins University Press, 2012).

Brinkman, B. "'A Place Known to the World as Devonshire Street': Modernism, Commercialism, and the Poetry Bookshop," in H. Osborne (ed.), *The Rise of the Modernist Bookshop: Books and the Commerce of Culture in the Twentieth Century* (Farnham: Ashgate Publishing Ltd., 2015), pp.113–30.

The British Book Trade Directory 1933 (London: J. Whitaker & Sons, Ltd.).

Cambridge, Marshall Library of Economics, 'Minutes of the Society', Marsoc1.

Carpenter, M. *A Rebel in the Thirties* (Wivenhoe: Paperbag Book Club, 1976).

Census of the Islands, Guernsey, St. Peter Port (1911).

"A Challenge," *Twentieth Century*, 8 (October 1931).

Chambers, M. *Modernism, Periodicals, and Cultural Poetics* (London: Palgrave Macmillan, 2015).

Chartered Society of Massage and Medical Gymnastics: Register of Masseuses and Masseurs (London: Printed for the Society by the Campfield Press, St. Albans, 1934).

Chartered Society of Massage and Medical Gymnastics: Register of Masseuses and Masseurs: Directory of Members (London: Tavistock House (North), 1938).

Cocaign, E. "The Left's Bibliophilia in Interwar Britain: Assessing Booksellers' Role in the Battle of Ideas," *Twentieth Century Communism*, 4 (2012), pp.218–30.

Cole, M. *Books and the People* (London: The Hogarth Press, 1938).

Collier, P. *Modern Print Artefacts: Textual Materiality and Literary Value in British Print Culture, 1890-1930s* (Edinburgh: Edinburgh University Press, 2018).

Cooke, B. *The Blasphemy Depot: A Hundred Years of the Rationalist Press Association* (London: Rationalist Press Association, 2003).

Cooper, J. X. "Bringing the Modern to Market: The Case of Faber & Faber," in L. Jaillant (ed.), *Publishing Modernist Fiction and Poetry* (Edinburgh: Edinburgh University Press, 2019).

Cope, D. "Radical Bookshop History Project," www.leftontheshelf books.co.uk/ images/doc/Radical-Bookshops-Listing.pdf

Central Books: A Brief History 1939 to 1999 (London: Central Books Ltd., 1999).

Bibliography of the Communist Party of Great Britain (London: Lawrence and Wishart Ltd., 2016).

Cripps, L. *C.L.R. James: Memories and Commentaries* (New York: Cornwall Books, 1997).

Cunard, N. *These Were the Hours* (Carbondale: Southern Illinois University Press, 1969).

'David Archer Alderson Archer," Wellington College Register, 1859–1948.

"David Archer Alderson Archer," Matriculation record for Gonville and Caius College, ref. /TUT/01/01/09.

Delany, P. "Who Paid for Modernism?" in M. Woodmansee and M. Osteen (eds.), *The New Economic Criticism: Studies at the Intersection of Literature and Economics* (London: Routledge, 1999), pp.286–99.

"Dobb on Planning under Fascism: Wrong Article in Anti-Marxist Journal," *Daily Worker* (July 6, 1932), p.4.

Dobb, M. "Marxism and the Crisis," *Twentieth Century* 16 (June 1932), pp.1–5.

"Correspondence," *Twentieth Century* 16 (June 1932), p.24.

"Editorial," *Modern Quarterly*, 1.2 (March 1938), pp. 103–4.

Edwards, R. D. *Victor Gollancz: A Biography* (London: Victor Gollancz Ltd., 1987).

Electoral Register, Camberwell 1932 (London: Corporation of London Joint Archive Service, 1932).

Electoral Register, *Camberwell 1935* (London: Corporation of London Joint Archive Service, 1935).

England and Wales Register, Lancashire, Manchester 1939.

"Ethical Society Secretary Found Dead," *The Times* (August 16, 1932), p. 7.

Evans, J. R. "The Promethean Society: A Survey," *Twentieth Century* 1 (March 1931), pp.23–4.

Fabes, G. *The Romance of a Bookshop* (London: Privately printed, 1938).

Feather, J. *A History of British Publishing* (London: Routledge, 1988).

A History of British Publishing, 2nd ed. (London: Routledge, 2006).

Fraser, A. *Cromwell: The Lord Protector* (New York: Grove Press, 1973).

Fraser, R. *Night Thoughts: The Surreal Life of the Poet David Gascoyne* (Oxford: Oxford University Press, 2012).

The Chameleon Poet: A Life of George Barker (London: Pimlico, 2014).

Gascoyne, D. *Collected Journals* (London: Skoob Books Pub Ltd., 1991).

Gordon, L. *Nancy Cunard; Heiress, Muse, Political Idealist* (New York: Columbia University Press, 2009).

Grant, J. *Harold Monro and the Poetry Bookshop* (London: Routledge and Kegan Paul, 1967).

Grigson, G. *Recollections: Mainly of Artists and Writers* (London: Chatto & Windus, 1984).

Gross, R. A. "Giving in America: From Charity to Philanthropy," in L. J. Friedman and M. D. McGarvie (eds.), *Charity, Philanthropy, and Civility in American History* (Cambridge: Cambridge University Press, 2003), pp.29–48.

Halliday, N. V. *More Than a Bookshop: Zwemmer's and Art in the 20th Century* (London: Philip Wilson Publishers Ltd., 1991).

Hammill F. and Hussey, M. *Modernism's Print Cultures* (London: Bloomsbury, 2016).

Harding, J. *Criterion: Cultural Politics and Periodical Networks in Inter-War Britain* (Oxford: Oxford University Press, 2002).

Harrison, R., Woovlen, G., and Duncan, R. *The Warwick Guide to British Labour Periodicals, 1790–1970: A Check List* (Hassocks: The Harvester Press Ltd., 1977).

"Hauteville House," www.maisonsvictorhugo.paris.fr/fr/musee-collec tions/visite-de-hauteville-house-guernesey

Hawkins, D. *When I Was: A Memoir of the Years between the Wars* (London: Macmillan London Ltd., 1989).

Hayes, D. *East of Bloomsbury* (London: Camden History Society, 1998).

"Heavy Sentences on *Daily Worker* Sellers," *Daily Worker* (August 8, 1934), p. 3.

Hilliard, C. *To Exercise Our Talents: The Democratization of Writing in Britain* (Cambridge, MA: Harvard University Press, 2006).
  "The Literary Underground of the 1920s," *Social History* 33.2 (2008), pp. 164–82.

The History and Function of Cambridge House (Cambridge: Bowes and Bowes, 1934).

Hobday, C. *Edgell Rickword: A Poet at War* (Manchester: Carcanet Press Ltd., 1989).

Hodges, S. *Gollancz: The Story of a Publishing House, 1928–1978* (London: Victor Gollancz Ltd., 1978).

Høgsberg, C. *C.L.R. James in Imperial Britain* (Durham: Duke University Press, 2014).

Howarth, T. E. B. *Cambridge between the Wars* (London: William Collins Sons & Co. Ltd., 1978).

Huxley, A. 'The Bookshop', in *Limbo* (London: Chatto & Windus, 1920), pp. 259–68.

Ingram, K. *Rebel: The Short Life of Esmond Romilly* (London: Weidenfeld and Nicolson, 1985).

Jaillant, L. *Cheap Modernism: Expanding Markets, Publishers' Series, and the Avant-Garde* (Edinburgh: Edinburgh University Press, 2018).

Kelly, J. "David Abercrombie," *Phonetica* 50.1 (1993), pp.66–9.

Jebb, M. *Walkers* (London: Constable and Company Ltd., 1986).

Joy, T. *The Bookselling Business* (London: Pitman Publishing, 1974).

'The Last Will and Testament of Samuel Frank Alderson Archer', District Probate Registry at Gloucester (05 September 2018).

Leavis, Q. D. *Fiction and the Reading Public* (London: Pimlico, 2000).

"Left Book Club [advertisement]," *New Statesmen and Nation* (February 29, 1936), pp. 124–5.

"Left Book Club [advertisement]," *Left Review*, 2.12 (September 1936), p.658.

"Left Book Club Enrollment Form," *Daily Worker* (May 27, 1936), p. 3.

"London Scottsboro Appeal Committee," *The Daily Worker* (December 14, 1933), p.4.

Lowell, A. 'The Bookshop', *Poetry: A Magazine of Verse* 6 (September 1919), pp. 310–11.

Lucas, J. *The Left Book Club: An Historical Record* (London: Victor Gollancz Ltd., 1970).

Lycett, A. *Dylan Thomas: A New Life* (New York: The Overlook Press, 2004).

MacCarthy, F. *William Morris: A Life of Our Time* (London: Faber and Faber, 1994).

MacNiven, I. *Literchoor Is My Beat: A Life of James Laughlin* (New York: Farrar, Straus and Giroux, 2014).

Mandler, P. "Good Reading for the Million: The 'Paperback Revolution' and the Co-Production of Academic Knowledge in Mid-Twentieth Century Britain and America," *Past and Present* 24.1 (August 2019), pp. 235–69.

Mengham, R. "Nationalist Papers Please Reprint," in P. Brooker and A. Thacker (eds.), *The Oxford Critical and Cultural History of Modernist Magazines*, Vol. 1: *Britain and Ireland, 1880–1950* (New York: Oxford University Press, 2007), pp. 688–703.

Meyers, J. *Resurrections: Authors, Heroes – and a Spy* (Charlottesville: University of Virginia Press, 2018).

"Mr. *Churchill's* Nephew Vanishes from Public School: 'Under the Influence of London Communists,' Says Mother," *Daily Express*, 10.532, (February 10, 1934), p.1.

Mumby F. and Norrie, I. *Publishing and Bookselling* (London: Jonathan Cape Ltd., 1974).

Murry, J. M. "Notes on Communism," *Twentieth Century* 13 (March 1932), pp.3–5.

Nancy, J. L. *On the Commerce of Thinking: Of Bookshops and Bookstores* (New York: Fordham University Press, 2009).

'New Books', *Left News* 31 (November 1938), p.1065.

N.H.T.C.: Its Plans for 1931 (National Holiday Touring Club, Ltd., 1931).

Orwell, G. "Bookshop Memories," in P. Davison (ed.), *The Complete Works of George Orwell*, Vol. 10: *A Kind of Compulsion, 1903–1936* (London: Secker & Warburg, 2000), pp. 510–13.

Osborne, H. "Introduction: Openings," in H. Osborne (ed.), *The Rise of the Modernist Bookshop: Books and the Commerce of Culture in the Twentieth Century* (Farnham: Ashgate Publishing Ltd., 2015), pp. 1–13.

"Counter-Space in Charles Lahr's Progressive Bookshop," in H. Osborne (ed.), *The Rise of the Modernist Bookshop: Books and the Commerce of Culture in the Twentieth Century* (Farnham. Ashgate Publishing Ltd., 2015), pp. 131–61.

Overy, R. *The Morbid Age: Britain and the Crisis of Civilization, 1919–1939* (London: Penguin Books, 2010).

Pendle, G., Evans, J. R., and Barraud, E. M. "The Revolt of Youth," *Everyman*, 3.74 (June 26, 1930), p.684.

Pendle, G., Evans, J. R., and Barraud, E. M. "The Revolt of Youth," *Everyman*, 3.76 (July 10, 1930), p.716.

Pennybacker, S. *From Scottsboro to Munich: Race and Political Culture in 1930s Britain* (Princeton: Princeton University Press, 2009).

Plant, M. *The English Book Trade; An Economic History of the Making and Sale of Books* (London: George Allen & Unwin Ltd., 1939).

Poole, P. J. "Sunday Ramble," *Daily Worker* (May 14, 1936), p.6.

Rainey, L. *Institutions of Modernism: Literary Elites and Public Culture* (New Haven: Yale University Press, 1998).

"The Cultural Economy of Modernism," in M. Levenson (ed.), *The Cambridge Companion to Modernism* (Cambridge: Cambridge University Press, 1999), pp.33–69.

The Road to '37: An Exhibition (London: Collet's Bookshops, 1937).

Romilly, G. and Romilly, E. *Out of Bounds: The Education of Giles Romilly and Esmond Romilly* (London: Hamish Hamilton Ltd., 1935).

Salton-Cox, G. *Queer Communism and the Ministry of Love: Sexual Revolution in British Writing of the 1930s* (Edinburgh: Edinburgh University Press, 2018).

"Samuel Frank Alderson Archer," *The London Gazette* (December 24, 1912), p. 9828.

Samuel, R. "Theatre and Socialism in Britain (1880–1935)," in R. Samuel, E. MacColl, and S. Cosgrove (eds.), *Theatre of the Left, 1880–1935: Workers' Theatre Movements in Britain and America* (London: Routledge and Kegan Paul, 1985), pp.3–73.

Sanders, F. *British Book Trade Organization: A Report on the Work of the Joint Committee* (London: George Allen & Unwin Ltd., 1939).

Saville, J. "Eva Collet Reckitt: Communist Bookseller," in J. M. Bellamy and J. Saville (eds.), *Dictionary of Labour Biography*, Vol. 9 (Houndmills: Macmillan, 1993), pp.239–43.

Sawaya, F. "Philanthropy and Transatlantic Print Culture," in A. Ardis and P. Collier (eds.), *Transatlantic Print Cultures, 1880–1940: Emerging*

Media, Emerging Modernisms (Houndsmills: Palgrave Macmillan, 2008), pp.83–97.

Sawaya, F. *The Difficult Art of Giving: Patronage, Philanthropy, and the American Literary Market* (Philadelphia: University of Pennsylvania Press, 2014).

Schleifer, R. *A Political Economy of Modernism: Literature, Post-Classical Economics, and the Lower Middle-Class* (Cambridge: Cambridge University Press, 2018).

"Scottsboro Boys Appeal," *The Daily Worker* (March 2, 1934), p.1.

"The Scottsboro Defense Committee Presents Famous Negro Artistes in an All-Star Entertainment," *The Daily Worker* (May 23, 1935), p.2.

Sisman, A. *John le Carré: A Biography* (New York: HarperCollins, 2015).

"Statement of Aims," *Modern Quarterly* 1.1 (January 1938), p.3.

Swinnerton, F. *Authors and the Book Trade* (London: Gerald Howe Ltd., 1932).

Symons, J. *The Thirties: A Dream Revolved* (London: Faber and Faber Ltd., 1960).

Taraporevala, R. J. *Competition and Its Control in the British Book Trade, 1850–1939* (London: Pitman Publishing, 1973).

Thacker, A. "'A True Magic Chamber': The Public Face of the Modernist Bookshop," *Modernist Cultures*, 11.3 (2016), pp.429–51.

"Circulating Literature: Libraries, Bookshops, and Book Clubs," in B. Kohlmann and M. Taunton (eds.), *A History of 1930s British Literature* (Cambridge: Cambridge University Press, 2019), pp.89–104.

Toynbee, P. *Friends Apart: A Memoir of Esmond Romilly & Jasper Ridley in the Thirties*, 2nd ed. (London: Sidgwick and Jackson, 1980).

Trease, G. *A Whiff of Burnt Boats* (London: Macmillan and Co. Ltd., 1971).

Unwin, S. *The Truth About Publishing* (London: George Allen and Unwin Ltd., 1926).

Wade, R. "The Parton Street Poets," *Poetry Review*, 54.4 (Winter 1963–4), pp. 290–7.

Weinreb, B. "No. 4 Parton Street," *Camden History Review* 13 (1985), pp. 15–18.

West, N. *Mask: MI5's Penetration of the Communist Party of Great Britain* (London: Routledge, 2012).

Wicke, J. "Coterie Consumption: Bloomsbury, Keynes, and Modernism as Marketing," in K. J. Dettmar and S. Watt (eds.), *Marketing Modernisms: Self- Promotion, Canonization, Rereading* (Ann Arbor: University of Michigan Press, 1996), pp. 109–32.

Worley, M. *Labour Inside the Gate: A History of the British Labour Party between the Wars* (London: I. B. Tauris & Co. Ltd., 2008).

"Writers' International (British Section)," *Left Review* 1.1 (October 1934), p. 38.

Acknowledgments

This book is dedicated to John and Dana Rigney (The Second Reader Bookshop) and Jonathon Welch (Talking Leaves Books), Buffalo, New York, booksellers who taught me the trade and whose friendship I continue to cherish. And to the late Sean Bonney: it was a unique pleasure knowing him.

I would like to thank several people who made this research possible. Dave Cope (Left on the Shelf Books) for answering my questions and for his exhaustive research documenting radical booksellers and publishers, and to Sarah Wise, Natasha de Chroustchoff, Julian Rota, and Julie Eaton, for their kind answers to my queries. Thanks to the staff at Wellington College, Gonville and Caius College, and the Marshall Library at Cambridge University, the Women's Library Reading Room at the London School of Economics, the Beinecke Rare Book and Manuscript Library at Yale University, the Centre for Research Collections at Edinburgh University, the Marx Memorial Library, the Camden Local Studies and Archives Centre, the London Metropolitan Archives, the National Archives (UK), the British Library, and the South Place Ethical Society for their help answering questions, finding materials, making scans, and granting permissions. A special thank you to Joy Bloomfield of the Wiltshire and Swindon History Centre for her assistance with the Archer family materials.

Thank you to the participants of the 2019 British Association for Modernist Studies conference where material comprising part of the first section was presented, especially to the audience members who asked productive questions, and my co-panelists, Beci Carver and Michael McCluskey, who helped me improve my idea. Additional thanks to colleagues on Twitter for the support and unexpected, if welcome, information, especially those who posted under the hashtag #ModWrite.

Finally, I finished this work during a very hectic year for our family. I appreciate Karolina Krasuska and our daughters' patience and support while I saw this through, and I love them all the more for it. Special thanks to my late uncle Robert Chambers, who showed me from an early age the privilege and fun of being an educator.

Cambridge Elements $\equiv$

Publishing and Book Culture

SERIES EDITOR

Samantha Rayner
University College London

Samantha Rayner is a Reader in UCL's Department of Information Studies. She is also Director of UCL's Centre for Publishing, co-Director of the Bloomsbury CHAPTER (Communication History, Authorship, Publishing, Textual Editing and Reading) and co-editor of the Academic Book of the Future BOOC (Book as Open Online Content) with UCL Press.

ASSOCIATE EDITOR

Leah Tether
University of Bristol

Leah Tether is Professor of Medieval Literature and Publishing at the University of Bristol. With an academic background in medieval French and English literature and a professional background in trade publishing, Leah has combined her expertise and developed an international research profile in book and publishing history from manuscript to digital.

About the Series

This series aims to fill the demand for easily accessible, quality texts available for teaching and research in the diverse and dynamic fields of Publishing and Book Culture. Rigorously researched and peer-reviewed Elements will be published under themes, or 'Gatherings'. These Elements should be the first check point for researchers or students working on that area of publishing and book trade history and practice: we hope that, situated so logically at Cambridge University Press, where academic publishing in the UK began, it will develop to create an unrivalled space where these histories and practices can be investigated and preserved.

Cambridge Elements ☰

Publishing and Book Culture
Bookshops and Bookselling

Gathering Editor: Eben Muse

Eben Muse is Senior Lecturer in Digital Media at Bangor University and co-Director of the Stephen Colclough Centre for the History and Culture of the Book. He studies the impact of digital technologies on the cultural and commercial space of bookselling, and he is part-owner of a used bookstore in the United States.

ELEMENTS IN THE GATHERING

Printed in the United States
By Bookmasters